DRESS CODE

Ending Fashion Anarchy

EVE MICHAELS

JACQUIE JORDAN, INC.

DRESS CODE: ENDING FASHION ANARCHY

Published by Jacquie Jordan Inc.

Copyright © 2012 by Eve Michaels

Author Photos by Starla Fortunato
Illustrations by Paula Cobian
Front cover design by Darice Fisher and Jonathan Fong
Interior book design by Barbara Aronica-Buck
Edited by Margie Kaye and Jackie Petruzzelli

ISBN 13 978-098193118-0

www.TVGuestpert.com
www.JacquieJordanIncPublishing.com

All rights reserved. No part of this publication may be reproduced, stored in a retrieval system, or transmitted, in any form or by any means, electronic, mechanical, photocopying, recording, or otherwise, without prior written permission of the publisher.

First Hardcover Printing June 2012

Printed in the United States of America
10 9 8 7 6 5 4 3 2 1

CONTENTS

ACKNOWLEDGMENTS	v
DEDICATION	ix
CHAPTER ONE: The Problem in America	1
CHAPTER TWO: My Truth About Beauty	16
CHAPTER THREE: Comfort and Style are Not Enemies	28
CHAPTER FOUR: The Five Stages of Grieving	35
CHAPTER FIVE: A Great Image is a Way of Life!	49
CHAPTER SIX: Knowing What Makes You Special	57
CHAPTER SEVEN: Your Unique Facial Shape and Body Proportions	73
CHAPTER EIGHT: How to Shop, Follow Trends and Get the Most from Your Wardrobe	95
CHAPTER NINE: The Smart Shopper's Guide to Investing in Your Wardrobe Portfolio	106
CHAPTER TEN: Head to Toe Beauty	116
CHAPTER ELEVEN: Great Grooming and Understanding Underwear	125
CHAPTER TWELVE: Personal Dress Code Commitment	132
EPILOGUE: Instituting Modern Dress Codes and Guidelines	139
ABOUT THE AUTHOR	151

ACKNOWLEDGMENTS

This book is the culmination of my life's work, experiences, and spiritual study. Writing it has been an incredible journey, and I have many wonderful people to thank for their guidance and help towards the making of *Dress Code: Ending Fashion Anarchy* a reality.

I am the woman I am and can do what I do because of my deep faith in and love of God, Spirit and My Angels, who are always with me, guiding me, and illuminating my path. Without them I would be nothing. They add grace, humility and beauty to everything I do.

Thank you to my loving husband, Robert Stoltz, who has hugged me through every setback and celebrated every triumph. He has been my greatest advocate, unshakeable in his belief that the world needs what I have to share. He is a man of honor and intelligence with a kind and gentle heart and I love him dearly.

To all of my amazing children who push my buttons and make me strive for excellence, I thank them with all my heart. They are treasures to me, each and every one of them. To my firstborn, Marissa who opened my eyes to Spirit with her special gifts and deep love and her husband, Avi, a true stand-up guy and wonderful son-in-law and our future granddaughter, June Elizabeth due to be born before this book! To my younger daughter, Nico, whose tenacity, love of success, and individuality has pushed me to "just do it" and never give up. To my son, Mitchell, who inspired me to become my own "before and after" and whose passion for fitness and excellence keeps inspiring my own. To my stepdaughter, Allison, my Gemini book end whose love of shopping may even exceed my own. And to my stepson, Jeff, whose love of beautiful women reminds me of my father, Nathan Burstyn. I am who I am in large part because of my father, who loved beauty and style. I learned how to overcome adversity and "never let myself down" because of his tenacity, faith and hope. My father, blessed be his memory, was my best friend and my rock. My family is my anchor.

To my many Beauty Boot Camp and Men's Overhaul Program students who shared their insights and experiences with me, I appreciate you. You have given me years of wisdom and raised my awareness of how powerful beauty and image are when put into practice. For all the years of joyful teaching, I thank you for giving me someone to teach. To my many private clients, thank you for allowing me to share my knowledge and enhance your lives as you have equally enhanced mine.

To Jacquie Jordan, my publisher and mentor. It was Jacquie's idea for me to write this book and it was Jacquie who brought out the best in me and pushed me to a higher level of excellence than I ever dreamed possible. Working with Jacquie and her team is a miracle in motion. I am eternally grateful for all of their patience and countless hours of tireless help. Jacquie and her entire TVGuestpert team have been a huge source of clarity and inspiration for my work. I feel compelled to name the people from TVG, who have had an important role in the creation of this book. Richard Waner, who holds the vision for my success and the big picture for the marketing of my business and talents. Darice Fisher and Jonathan Fong, lead graphic artists, who created the cover of this book, my website and all of my marketing materials. Stephanie Cobian who helped produce my radio show, is my constant cheerleader and keeper of the TVG gates. Elisa Schwartz, who was the first producer to recognize my talents and my vision. Elisa has mentored me and it was Elisa who connected Jacquie and me for which I am ever grateful. Jane Shayne who gets the media to see my talents in radio, print and interviews and Clayton Spires for his IT genius. Alexia Haidos, who is intent on getting my message out to the world. Thank you TVG for seeing my successes before I do and in ways I never imagined.

Many thanks also to Margie Kaye, for keeping me on my writing path and making certain my writing flowed in the most understandable way. Margie never lost patience with my "flash back" style of writing and applauded my desire to write this book in my authentic voice.

I could not be the woman I am without the help and guidance of my spiritual healers and teachers. I give humble thanks to Teresa Tharp, Trish Loar, and Matthew Love. Their talents truly are a gift from God and they keep me evolving into my best authentic self. They continually show me the light and the way, keeping me connected to Spirit. There are no words to express the many blessings you have bestowed upon me and countless others you have so tirelessly helped.

For over twenty years, I have studied the writings and wise teachings of Dr. Wayne Dyer, Esther and Jerry Hicks/Abraham, Don Miguel Ruiz, Neale Donald Walsch, Marianne Williamson, Dr. David Hawkins, Napoleon Hill, Norman Vincent Peale, Deepak Chopra, Louise Hay, Mother Teresa, and Doreen Virtue. A special acknowledgement to Reverend Michael Bernard Beckwith of Agape Spiritual Center in Los Angeles, California where I was a member for over ten years. His teachings, sermons, classes and silent meditation retreats continue to be a life-changing and powerful source of spiritual guidance filled with love.

To the very first person who recognized my talents as a media personality, Gemma Cunningham. I am grateful for her continual faith in my work.

Truthfully, what would any woman be without her hairdresser? Craig Piatti, my very talented and kind hairdresser and friend has helped me fall in love with my hair, showing me that my naturally curly hair is beautiful worn just as is or blown out straight. Craig always tells me if a woman feels good about the way she looks, she will walk into a room with confidence, no matter what the trend. Confidence, he says, trumps a bad hair day. "Just let your beautiful face shine, baby!" and I do that more now because of Craig.

To all my friends, old and new, thank you for inspiring me with your kindness, creativity, courage and love of God. Your friendships help me celebrate life and give it a richer meaning. I love each and every one of you. Sally Warshawsky (my surrogate mother), Ana Weber (who encouraged me to show the world my before and after), Caroline Shrednick (who told me I must write the truth about my life). To my newer friends: Susan and Jeff Merrick, Lyn and Jerry Bresnahan, Renee Huggans, Aileen Krassner and Joe Doug Griffin, Ed Barkley and Jim Rebman, Candace and Michael Partridge, Susan and Craig Lubin, JK and Lacy Hunt, Patricia and David Flanary, Cord Shiflet, Ian Stonington, and Krystina Trzaskowki and William Robinson III.

A special mention to my brother-in-law and his wife: Richard and Helena Stoltz. They are the epitomy of decency, kindness, and loyalty. My husband and I love them deeply. And to their children Jason and Melissa Stoltz (and their children Jacob and Ariel), Rebecca Stoltz Tiano and Joe Tiano (and their baby Alexander), you are all very special to us, as is the entire Stoltz family.

DEDICATION

Dress Code: Ending Fashion Anarchy is dedicated to my loving, patient husband Robert whose constant belief in my message has sustained me and fed my soul. The sacred space he created for me allowed me to make this passionate endeavor of mine possible.

This book is also dedicated to our children: Marissa, Nicole, Mitchell, Avi, Jeffrey and Allison, all of whom have encouraged me to never give up on my dreams.

The beauty and love of my family have added grace and meaning to my life and work.

Most of all, this book is dedicated to all seekers of beauty whose love of it heals and illuminates their way.

CHAPTER ONE

The Problem in America

Most people are familiar with the iconic phrase, "Houston, we have a problem," as the astronauts aboard Apollo 13 stated from space to the command center in Houston in 1970 ...

Well, I hate to break it to you. Fast forward three decades later, and we have a problem in *all* of America when it comes to our pursuit of beauty and all that it entails. You don't have to be a "rocket scientist" to figure this out. We have become a nation of people who have turned our backs on our appearance and our health and have entered a new frontier of complacency and neglect. This is how the rest of the world views us. Sadly, we have brought this mess upon ourselves.

Of course, I am not referring to everyone in this country. There are people who dress and groom well on a consistent basis (and take care of their health) but they are in the minority and their numbers seem to be diminishing, as the desire to be "comfortable" at any cost is taking over our population! Haven't we learned that most things worth having don't come without effort, time and money? Is there anything in this world that we can neglect and still have a positive outcome? Our personal appearance is the same. If we don't take good care of it, it will quickly go to seed. Instead of looking like beautiful blooms, we will look like a bunch of weeds, and it is precisely this lack of care that is affecting our psyche as a nation. It is diminishing our personal power and creating a general malaise.

You may be thinking that our looking unkempt and slovenly has nothing to do with the present economic problems in our country. But from all I have studied over the last twenty years about quantum physics and the laws of attraction, I believe that how we are caring for ourselves individually has a direct correlation to the mess we are in collectively. We seem to be unwilling to do what it takes to uplift ourselves, and to have personal pride and self-respect.

This is being reflected in our national mood. We are looking to the government to do for us what we are unwilling to do: comport ourselves with dignity and pride, care for our health, and do what it takes to succeed; none of which may be "comfortable" at the onset, but will make us much more secure and comfortable later. Taking the easy way out usually proves more difficult in the long run. Doing what is difficult now will make our lives better in the future.

Having a great image is so crucial to our morale and performance that I will boldly tell you that being beautiful is good for our country! It is the patriotic thing to do. We **are** our country! Each and every American represents an important part of the whole. Every time we travel, or do business, we represent the American people. We are all the microcosm of the macrocosm. Our role individually is just as important to our nation as the government, because "We The People" **are** "The People of This Great Nation." How we present ourselves matters! We need to wake up!!

As a nation, we Americans used to know this. We used to take pride in our appearance and we understood the expectations to dress and conduct ourselves to a certain standard. While we have never placed the importance on style that the Europeans do, we cared about our image nonetheless. We knew that image was important. Why we don't know it now is amazing to me. I am ashamed of how slovenly we have become. And I am saddened that no one seems to be talking about this as if it's politically incorrect to acknowledge what's happened to us. What makes me sadder is that for those who do want to improve their image, they are hard pressed to find someone or somewhere to teach them the skills they need. Image consultants are few and far between.

The demise of fashion has happened slowly and insidiously over time. The first famous person that I remember tossing out the dress code was movie director Steven Spielberg. He shook up the corporate world by becoming a multi-millionaire and a global film mogul while wearing his grungy baseball cap, logo t-shirt, denims, and athletic shoes. His overly casual (might I dare to say sloppy) appearance became almost as famous as his movies. Rumor has it that in the 90s he went to the Georges Cinq Hotel in Paris with his entourage where he had reservations to stay. The management went into an uproar that a guest could even walk into their hotel dressed so inappropriately and wanted him thrown out. However, after they found out it was 'Monsieur Spielberg', they retreated.

Soon, it seemed as if most people in this country dreamed of attaining the

Spielberg ideal: a super casual appearance coupled with loads of money and success. Maybe that's when the belief that comfort and style are enemies started in this country. Sadly, what most people didn't realize is that there are few men like Spielberg. For most of us, our image matters … more than we realize.

Another world famous man that influenced how corporate America dresses was Steve Jobs. While Steve seemed to have impeccable grooming, he bucked the system when he exchanged his suit for his iconic black turtlenecks tucked into denims with a belt. This image worked well for him as an innovator, genius and forward thinker. Steve's streamlined, stark and simple appearance matched the look of the products he launched. But sadly again too many people felt they could emulate his style and become a billionaire. In reality, few people can. A person like Steve Jobs is born maybe once in a generation. Sometimes an individual's style does not work for the masses.

As the world of technology grew and with it the advent of the stay-at-home entrepreneurs, the "techie" style of NO STYLE was born. The "who cares, no one sees me" sweats and tees, pajamas and slippers, unshaven, no makeup, messy hair, unkempt look became the depressing mode of dress for too many people in this country. And again, people thought this had no effect on their productivity or morale. Well guess what? The whole world doesn't dress techie and even techies need to know when it's time to dress up!

At first the demise of appearance and grooming was slow to be seen. Over a period of almost three decades, the decline is now evident and dramatic. The role models of image have mostly disappeared and with them, the finishing schools and the courses that taught people how to dress well. There are no courses taught to us in high school on this subject and none in universities. It's definitely not being taught anymore in our homes (or seemingly in very few). The ramification of this is that unless we are taught how to dress well at home or at school, few of us ever have a chance to learn this vital skill elsewhere.

It's incredible but most people don't even know their own facial shape, body proportions, or what colors flatter them; basic knowledge that every person should understand. This lack of knowledge coupled with the lack of dress codes (knowing what's expected of our image) turns dressing for many into an act of frustration, with hit or miss results. Thousands upon thousands of dollars are misspent on clothing, shoes and accessories that are never worn.

Or worse, spent on clothing that has a negative effect instead of a positive one: the result of which can cost us a long overdue promotion at work, missed sales, or even our jobs.

We used to have dress codes. Up until the 90s, we had dress codes at work, at restaurants, houses of worship, theatres and for social occasions. We knew the rules and we knew what was expected of us. Fast forward twenty years and we have fashion anarchy! Most people don't know how to dress appropriately anymore. People show up at work dressing like they are ready to mow the lawn or on the other extreme, dressed like they are ready to go clubbing. Many people go to the theatre in flip-flops and rumpled shorts. Logo t-shirts have replaced nice shirts and blouses. We think that anything goes as long as we cover our naked bodies. Nothing could be further from the truth!

The truth is that in this country, where we are overly concerned with being politically correct and are highly litigious, people are afraid to tell us that our sloppy appearance, poor grooming and lack of manners is costing us our job or our promotion. Not to mention our standing in this world as business is now mostly conducted worldwide. Other nations are scratching their heads in amazement when they meet us wondering why seemingly "successful Americans" look like they just rolled out of bed. To many of us, we do seem to be asleep at the wheel and no one is willing to stand up and shine a spotlight on this. We are afraid as a nation to talk about how slovenly the majority of us have become and how depressing it is.

I recently had the pleasure of interviewing Roy Cohen during a recent broadcast of The Eve Michaels Radio Show 1290AM Santa Barbara. He is a corporate career coach and author. He expressed his views on the importance of having the right image to compete. Roy went on to say that people in the corporate world need to "dress appropriately for the venue they're in." He also said that "in the current economic environment, power and energy need to be conveyed through one's appearance and style." Mr. Cohen said that a person needs to use good judgment as to whether he is wearing the right clothing for the right setting. "It's about exercising good judgment." Combine the lack of concern of appearance with the lack of knowledge of how to dress well, with a lack of fashion guidelines, and the result is fashion anarchy.

What's worse is that ever since 2008, our country has been in an economic slump. This gives people more reason to neglect their appearance, especially since they haven't seen the value in bettering their looks when the economy was good! But I am here to tell you that this is precisely the time to dig deeper into our pockets and clean up our act! I'm not talking just about spending on clothes. I am talking about getting a good haircut, grooming ourselves and taking our appearance up a notch! Why? Because we live in a globalized economy and we're competing worldwide for business. The rest of the modern world is taking their image more seriously and they see it as the competitive edge. They don't understand why we have become so complacent. We have to acknowledge the fact that we *are* competing with other countries for business and we have to look like we're on our A-game in every way.

For those of you who don't care about globalization and whose businesses are totally domestic, keep in mind that your own career success and personal life will be enhanced by improving your style and image. This can be the competitive edge that many Americans are searching for and it is also one of the most overlooked aspects of success.

We Americans tend to be isolationists. We have a tendency to hide our heads in the sand and think that what we do has no effect on how the world views us. This "we can do whatever we want and not care what the rest of the world is doing" kind of attitude has gotten us into big trouble before. We can't afford to be ostriches about anything again.

We tend to be naïve. We all know that when we look better, we feel better. We also get treated a whole lot better. So if we want the respect of other nations and our peers, we must look respectable! It begins with each and every one of us. No one else will give us respect if we don't give it to ourselves and a huge part of that is respecting how we show up in this world, everyday. Studies have shown that even people who do phone sales or run at-home based businesses actually sell better and do better when they dress professionally for their work. There is a huge difference in the energy and professionalism they exude. This is even more tangible in person.

President John F. Kennedy said in his famous inaugural speech, "Ask not what your country can do for you. Ask what you can do for your country!" Sometimes we don't think that we as individuals can make a difference. I am here to tell you that you can. Every improvement in this world begins with one thought, one emotion, one action and one person who is ready to stand up. Someone has to initiate the change and stop this madness. I am proud to do this for our nation and I hope you will all have the courage and tenacity to join me in this endeavor.

How will we begin to turn this around? By simply improving our image and manners on a consistent basis. People will begin to notice how nice you look, and believe me they will start to think more about cleaning up their appearance. Every person can have an affect, on average, on at least 100 people to look and act better themselves by having chosen to better their own image. At least ten people you know will start trying to look better, dress better and care more about themselves just because you did. Therefore, exponentially, you will have impacted many lives, perhaps never even realizing it. Why? Slowly, but surely we will start stepping into the light, boosting our morale, gaining positive momentum and turning this mess around.

There is something else very interesting that happens when we look better. We start to see something positive happening in our life. We look in the mirror and we see positive changes occurring. This leads us to believe that things are getting better. Our looking better has a direct effect on how we are treated. As we get treated better, we feel better and the positive cycle of success has begun. I know this works, because I have been helping people do just that for over thirty years!

Can you imagine for a moment that President Obama would visit other nations while dressed in a crumpled logo t-shirt, shorts and sandals? Well, why not? We know he's intelligent. We know he's powerful. We know who he is. So why doesn't he dress that way? He doesn't because he understands the power of image and self-respect. He dresses in a manner that is consistent with who he is, the job he has and the message he is sending. You would never ever have to tell the President or the First Lady the importance and power of image. Never!

Did you know that you can't get a good job in France unless you look good? That's because the French believe if someone cannot be attractive physically, then he/she can't possibly be intelligent enough to handle the job at hand! Also in France, if you don't dress nicely and are not well groomed, they will refuse to serve you in a restaurant. That's how much they value appearance. They are not shallow. They place a high value on the intellect, which they feel goes hand in hand with one's appearance. In Mexico, the wait staff dresses better than most of our bank tellers here in the United States! Even the lowest level entry professional employee wears clothes that are pressed and starched, with shoes polished and an overall attention to every grooming detail. As a nation, they take their image seriously. To them it is a matter of great pride.

In Italy, the Italians seem to ooze style, no matter where they go. Even their Gondola drivers look like they fell out of GQ Magazine! In Japan, style is King!! The Japanese will do anything to have beautiful skin, hair, nails and wear the latest clothing styles. They have such a deep appreciation of beauty. In Russia, a woman won't even take out her garbage without lipstick and high heels. Neither will the women in Buenos Aires, Argentina. But in our country many women will go outside barely dressed, some in their robes and pajamas, looking as if they literally ran out of the house. Shame on us! In Africa, even the tribes place a premium on beauty, when many other key elements in their lives are lacking, such as food and shelter for starters. They decorate their bodies in brightly colored garb, tribal beads, head dresses, customary markings and piercings to honor the beauty that represents their culture. Where is the honor in ours?

Several years ago, Sharon, a client of mine came to my image studio and brought me a poem as a present. She said that it represented to her all that I was teaching, and more. She felt it would be beneficial for me to share it with my clients before they worked with me. As I slowly read each word, my eyes welled with tears. I gazed up from the page and whispered, "Thank you, Sharon," my voice cracking with emotion. It was a poem by Marianne Williamson entitled *Our Greatest Fear*. In this poem, she speaks about how we are afraid to shine our light. We are afraid to be glorious and fabulous. She explains that beauty is our birthright and that we were born to be magnificent. I was deep in thought. The revelation came! Yes, yes, that's it! We are afraid to shine our light! We are afraid to let people see the real beauty in us. Why? I wondered. I had to know. And so began my twenty year search to find out what is it about our culture that tells us to dim our light? I hand the boot camp attendees a photo copy of the poem. *"Just take it in,"* I tell them. Then we talk through the concepts. What I found is that the poem puts an arrow through the heart of the issue here. We're not afraid to fail, we are afraid of how fabulous we are. And how powerful we can be.

Through teaching my Beauty Boot Camps and Men's Overhaul Programs, I began to figure out what this fear was all about. A lot of it stems from negative messaging about image from our childhoods. It comes from our parents telling us that caring too much about how we look wasn't the "Christian thing to do," or Jewish families saying, "We don't waste money on these kinds of things. All you need is a good education. Just be clean, that's all." In my opinion what ended up happening, is that many people consciously or unconsciously, for the sake of "fitting in" aimed for the lowest common denominator instead of the highest. We need to reverse that, if enough of us aim for the higher common denominator, then many of the rest will follow. For those of you who join me in raising the common denominator to a much higher standard, you will find that your happiness and success will be enhanced.

A large percentage of Americans were taught that it's vain to look good. Even worse, we think people won't like us if we stand out. We were taunted, "Who do you think you are, Missy? Are you a snob? Do you think you are better than everyone? You should save your money, not spend it on frivolous things like expensive clothing!" This *negative messaging taught many of us to attach something bad to looking good.* This goes against our innate nature as human beings to be beautiful.

For those people who wanted to stand out in a positive way, they didn't always know how. There is prejudice in this country against people who dress well. We were told not to be "show offs." Suffice it to say, as a nation, we have attached many negatives to looking good. Yet I will say that it is impossible to dim our soul's true nature, which is to seek out, respond to, and express beauty.

I also discovered from teaching my boot camps that approximately one-third of women in the United States have been sexually abused or molested, so many women are afraid to draw positive attention to their appearance. They hide their beauty behind baggy shapeless clothing. Between the women who have been sexually abused and the others who have been persuaded to look plain, no wonder we are afraid to be fabulous! What about men? They were taught that money is power, but not enough parents told them they also needed to look powerful!

For the small percentage who try to look great, they often face ridicule that is born out of ignorance; ignorance about the power of dressing well. People who look good often face jealousy and envy, so don't expect applause from others in the beginning, until you can learn to give it to yourself.

From the moment I read *Our Greatest Fear*, I decided to have every client of mine read it before I began working with them. I have included it in my workbooks and read it to my Beauty Boot Camp students at the beginning of every workshop. I read it onstage at my seminars; the crowds applaud. I read it often to remind myself of what I do and what I am trying to accomplish; to let my light shine and in doing so, give others permission to do the same. To this very day, that poem gives me chills every time I read it. Every time I read it to others there are tears. They are speechless. You can just feel the reaction in the room. It is palpable. It strikes a nerve and helps me set the right ideas and sentiments in motion.

"*I applaud all of you for having the courage to be here today at my New York Beauty Boot Bamp. I applaud you for having the courage to want to learn the skills to better yourselves and to do what it takes to improve your image. It especially takes courage to want to improve your image in this country, where the standard for dress and grooming is quite possibly the lowest standard in modernized societies! This saddens me, because letting go of one's image is a form of depression,*" I say to my new Beauty Boot Camp students as they sit wide-eyed, giving me their utmost attention. For a brief moment I think about my own mother and how her tragic accident caused her to stop caring about her appearance ...

"*My gift is that I can see the beauty in all of you. I can see your potential. Most of you see only what your mirror reflects back to you,*" I say as I gaze intently in their eyes.

"*You often see the worst in yourselves and I see the best. Most importantly, I see what you can be. I see how fabulous you all are! I see it for you, until you can see it for yourselves. It is my goal to help each and every one of you learn how to express your unique beauty. I am here to teach you how to let your light shine,*" I tell them.

"*You see, when you say one thing, but your image says another, there is a disconnect which lowers your energy/vibration because you feel trapped inside an image that doesn't harmonize with who you truly are. As a result, people don't get who you are and they don't treat you the way you wish to be treated. What happens is that you get received in the way you are perceived. Most people don't realize that this is in their control.*"

I can see the wheels begin to turn in my students as they focus on what I am saying. There is an awakening of their consciousness that excites me. I can feel the ideas I am sharing with them makes them think about image and beauty in a whole new way. I know their lives will never be the same after this workshop.

After years of teaching this subject, I know what it does and the magic that happens as a result of it. Every eye in the room is upon me as I continue.

"*All of you here at my Beauty Boot Camp are very special and important to me. I want you to know that when you graduate from my boot camp you will be my ambassadors of beauty! I take that very seriously. I assure you that when you return home people will treat you differently. Be sensitive to others' reactions and notice how you feel. Then watch how many people start to take better care of their image because you have. Like a ripple in a pond, you will see the positive effects you have on others. That is precisely what we need in this country to awaken Americans out of their image malaise. It must start somewhere, so why not here with you?*

"*The greatest change you will experience is that there will be a positive energy that will be unleashed in you that will be tangible. For when your image is out of harmony with who you are, a dissonance is created. You feel that blockage, as if your soul is imprisoned in an image that doesn't harmonize with who you really are. When your image and your essence are in harmony, a great positive power and energy aligns itself for your good. This energy will translate into the powerful cycle of success.*

"*I know that many of you feel guilty for even trying to enhance your beauty. I know there's a voice inside of you that says 'beauty is frivolous.' But true beauty is never frivolous, because next to love, beauty is one of the highest vibrations that exists. Our souls yearn to express beauty and be surrounded in beauty: in art, in music, in architecture, in design, and in ourselves. Even primitive cultures have important beauty rituals to decorate themselves. We yearn to feel beautiful. This is evidenced by the fact that almost every person feels better when he or she looks better,*" I say as I move around the room, stopping at each table.

"*We have always been known as innovators and leaders. America, the land of the free: where anyone can be rich and successful if they want to be. Freedom of speech and freedom of religion are ours for the taking. The entire world has looked to us, and longed to come here to America to fulfill their dreams. And I love that entrepreneurial spirit and can-do attitude about our country,*" I say to the proud faces.

"*However, it is not enough to be free and to lead the world in innovation. We must use our freedom to lead in all arenas; both personally and professionally. We have a duty, a responsibility to care about how people see us; in other words, to care about how we are perceived. It is time that we take personal responsibility for how we present ourselves and how we behave. No government can do this for us. We must do this for ourselves. That is precisely why I started teaching these Beauty Boot*

Camps. I realized that there are very few places for people to learn about image and dressing well. The majority of Americans don't teach image skills to their children anymore. Nor do they teach their children proper table manners. We should learn these skills in high school and college, as well as in our homes. It is my dream to get 'image courses' taught in schools and universities across our nation someday. I believe that we owe our children this knowledge and the basic teachings should be freely available to every American. We need to learn how to dress well and present ourselves in school and we need to reinforce these skills in the home," I say, emphatically.

"I understand that when you were lacking the knowledge and the know how to reinvent yourselves, it was easier to say it didn't matter. It was easier to tell yourself that being a good person was enough. But that's not the way it works in this physical world. We are spiritual beings having a physical experience. Before anyone gets to know us, they get to see us. Our image speaks volumes about who we are and people judge us by our appearance. As right or wrong as this may seem, it's true! I didn't invent the rules, I just know how to follow them," I insist.

We need to understand that how we are perceived is how we are received. In other words, our perception creates our reality. In our section about image, we will learn all about how to communicate effectively through our appearance.

Many of you may have watched the hit television show, Mad Men. That show is changing the face of fashion with its glamorous portrayal of the late 50s, early 60s era. It is interesting to note that during that time period and up through the 80s, personal style was very important to us as individuals and as a nation. The fashions were fabulous. Do I wish we dressed more like that? Yes and no. Yes to the elegance and no to the rigidity. That is because although people in that era looked very elegant and glamorous, the fashions were at the same time confining and rigid. Interestingly enough, so were the social mores of the early 60s. Rigid clothing, rigid mind-set. And during that time period where image mattered, there were also many social injustices. In this "land of the free" there was much discrimination against women, African Americans, Hispanics, Jews, the physically/mentally disabled and more. We were still fighting, as a nation, for civil rights, justice and equality.

Now fast forward to present time. We have come so far socially. In the process of finding our soul, we let go of our appearance. As our social consciousness became more just and liberal, our clothing relaxed as well. Then with the advent of the business casual dress code and internet based businesses, we began to take relaxed dressing to an extreme. So you could say we acted better and looked worse.

"That is why I said it takes courage for you to be here. Because although most people will admit that they want to look good, there is much prejudice against people who do. People may ridicule you for spending money to learn how to look your best. But I applaud you, because I know that having a great image will be the magical missing ingredient in many of your lives. The majority of people in our country haven't woken up to that fact. I think that's because so many people don't know how their image is affecting all aspects of their lives; professionally and personally!" I say.

I continue, "At the risk of being misunderstood, I will say that beauty must radiate from the inside out. It must come OUT and be expressed in a way that resonates to the individual, and in a form that communicates who he or she is and where he/she is going. You will learn the science behind image impact during our time together. However, for now, let's understand that in previous decades there was one universal stereotype for beautiful women: an oval face, an hourglass figure, fair skin, small nose, etc. Many of us born before 1960 remember that and how oppressing it was for most women. We have evolved in our thinking as we have globalized and now we recognize that there isn't only one formula for beauty. Beauty in its magnificence comes in all shapes, colors and sizes. It is expressed differently in every culture."

With a globalized society, comes globalized beauty and style. Always remember that beauty, like art, is unique and expressive, creative and uplifting. And more than anything, it feeds our souls. Its power is magnetic and draws us to feel its effect. We hunger for beauty: in us, as us, and around us. Never forget!

America, to its detriment, has had a long history of being isolationist. We tend to look inward and think what is happening in the rest of the world won't affect us here. We are largely ignorant of global geography and other cultures. We travel abroad and assume that things should be done "our way." Other countries find this attitude offensive just as they find our logo t-shirts, crumpled shorts and athletic shoes wandering around their cities to be ugly and out-of-place. We travel that way just the same, because we think it doesn't matter. We bemoan the fact that we get treated poorly. Trust me, if we all took more pride in our persons and dressed with respect for who we are and where we are going, the rest of the world would respect us more too. If you don't believe me, try it and see the difference.

"In fact, I want you to NOT BELIEVE anything I am teaching you for now.

That's right, you heard me. Don't believe a thing. Then try every theory. Test it all for yourselves. Test what I've taught you and watch the reactions. Notice the differences. Then and only then will these concepts become your truths.

"As Lester Levinson taught in his Sedona Method, 'Take it for checking.' Don't believe me? Try it for yourself."

We have died to have the freedoms that we have. It is not America that has made us look bad, we have made ourselves look bad and this reflects poorly not only on ourselves, but our nation. Freedom has enabled people to choose to be sloppy in their appearance. This is the same freedom that allows us as individuals to choose to improve our image. If enough people do this, then being stylish, well-groomed and well-dressed will soon become more of a national value; a national matter of pride.

I pull myself out of my reverie and continue, *"Did you know that in most countries, women can't wait to have the chance to put on makeup, fix their hair, take care of their complexions, wear beautiful clothing, walk in high heels and wear sexy lingerie? They appreciate the importance of having a great image and taking pride in their appearance. Great grooming is a given, not a chore. They look for every opportunity to present themselves well. Their motto is, why not? Of course, I want to look good!"* I say as some of the women look down.

"But in the United States, most women say 'Do I **have to?** Do I **have to** put on makeup? Do I **have to** dress nicely? Do I **have to** put on high heels? Do **I have to** get a manicure and pedicure?' In other countries most women are thrilled because they **get to** look good! While in our country, most women complain while asking why they **have to!**

"If we would only realize that saying '**I get to**' imbues the positive energy of gratitude into everything we do versus '**I have to,**' which makes everything we do seem like drudgery."

I was inspired by a sermon delivered by Reverend Michael Beckwith of the Agape Spiritual Center in Los Angeles. Reverend Beckwith shed light on the premise that it is the energy and the intention behind everything that creates the result and therefore, for example, we are lucky to **get to** pick up our children from school, because we are fortunate to have a family; we are lucky to **get to** clean the dishes after dinner because we have food to eat; we are lucky we **get to** dress with style, because we have clothes on our back. We **get to,** not we **have to!** What a brilliant way to see life!

We as a people have so much in this country; tremendous conveniences and vast wealth, and yet so many of us dress as if we were poor. Compared to many countries, most of us don't know what true poverty is! It seems that for many of us all that we care about is comfort, convenience and fast food. We care about quantity not quality. We have become an overweight and out of style nation. What happened to us as a people? When did we stop caring about our appearance, our education, and our health? When did beauty and other things of value stop being important and how did we get into this mess?

"*Obviously there are people who are stylish, slim, and in good health in this country. But they have become the minority instead of the majority. People from other nations come here for the first time, see us, and scratch their heads in disbelief. Over and over I hear them say, "How could this be? How can Americans look like this, and why? My boot camp students have been Russian, Japanese, German, Jamaican, South American, Canadian, French, Indian, Israeli and from every part of the world. The remarks I hear are always the same. They are shocked at how people, even people of means, dress so badly in this country. They ask why we don't care. They wonder what happened to us and why we allow this to be the norm.*"

You can hear a pin drop in the room. The nervous tension is thick as the women worry about what I will say about them. I feel for them. I realize that we women have been put down and criticized more than enough; by ourselves, by our parents, by our peers, and even by our husbands/partners. So I quickly try to assuage their fears and let them know that I am here to build them up and uplift them. Some of the women are still upset because I didn't allow them to wear denims, t-shirts, sweat pants or flip-flops to my seminar. I asked them to respect our dress code by dressing as if they were going on a first date or a job interview. At every single boot camp, a percentage of the women whine and complain that they don't own anything nice to wear. Unmoved we tell them, "Then go buy something." One would think it were torture to dress up a bit, really!

A person can look attractive on any budget. Money is not the issue. It rarely is, because in this country we have stylish clothing at every price point. Even during The Great Depression, when many people were starving they still managed to look presentable and decent. Even if they only had 1-2 outfits, they presented themselves well. The real issue here is the lack of *desire* to look good. It's precisely those people who have lost the desire to take care of their looks who use money or the lack of it as an excuse. So many people have forgotten about how much better they will get treated when they look good. Restaurants magically make a table available, hotels upgrade your room, flight attendants treat you nicer. Oh, and let's not forget that stores give you better service, all because you treated yourself with more respect! Why? Because people treat us for the large part consummate with how we treat ourselves.

"Before we truly begin this workshop, let's gather around and form a circle. Now let's join hands and close our eyes. Please take three deep cleansing breaths. Let out your fears and nervous tension … I want to thank every woman in this room for this opportunity to work with you. I want to uplift you and help you step into your unique beauty. I want you to know that this is a sacred place; a place where every woman will encourage one another to be her best and her most beautiful. There is great wisdom in this room. We will learn from one another in these next three to four days. Thank you for honoring this safe place. We will keep one another's confidence and trust. For many of you this will be the very first time that you will be in an environment where other women, total strangers, will celebrate one another's beauty. I ask you all to leave your egos outside of the building because this is not about your ego. It is about how you communicate with your image and the skills it takes to do that well."

The energy grows more positive in the room as eyes fill with emotion. After I finish, I instruct, *"You may now let go of your hands. Please stay in the circle and tell us the following: Your name, your age, if you are married or in a relationship, if you have children and their ages, where you live, what you do for a living, why you are here and what your goals are for this boot camp."*

My assistant writes down each woman's goals, because I know that their new image will help them reach those goals faster and more joyously than they ever imagined was possible. And I take that very, very seriously.

I smile as I look down at my high heeled red soled shoes and I remember a time, not so long ago, when I couldn't even afford new shoes, let alone the red soled, red carpet kind. I think about how far I have come and how many dreams have come true. Has it really been over thirty years that I have been trying to guide people to shine their own light? Yes, it has. Actually, this all began more than thirty years ago, when I was less than five years old. I first tried to heal my very own mother through beauty, as she was being treated in the state mental hospital.

CHAPTER TWO

My Truth About Beauty

When I was only a year and a half old, my mother's car went off a cliff. Her brain was permanently damaged and my life was forever changed.

"Mommy, please put on this lipstick. Please!" I cried at five years old. "Shave your legs, mommy. Put on this nice cream. You will feel better," I pleaded as I sorted through the bag of treats like a frenzied child on Halloween.

Every other week I walked to the beauty supply store by myself and picked out a beautiful new lipstick and nail polish for my mother. I always chose a bright, cheerful color. Let's see … *Petal Pink, Nectarine, Really Red* … these will do, I convinced myself.

"Little girl, where are your parents? Do they know you are here?" asked the owner of the store. I didn't reply. I was lost amidst the rows and rows of makeup and beauty products that enticed me with their hypnotic promises. I was so distracted I would not give her an answer. I was concentrating on making the right selection … the one that I thought would help heal my mother and make her normal again. Normal for me meant that she could come home. Normal meant that she would look like she did before the accident. Normal meant I would have a mother like all of my friends at school. Normal meant the stares and the whispers from "well intentioned" parents and neighbors would stop; the stares that said, "Poor Evie, she doesn't have a mother to raise her."

The doctors weren't making her better. So I believed that I could. I would make her mental illness go away. I would bring her beauty back. Even as a little girl, I thought that if mommy could start taking care of herself and look pretty again, she would get better.

As the car engine stopped, I cocked my head back and stared up at the ominous buildings. The state mental hospital was not a place that any five year-old would look forward to visiting, but for me it was another chance to help bring mommy home.

"You are so busted," I say as I toss the green and black ball to one of the ladies enrolled in my Beauty Boot Camp.

"What do you mean you don't have time to put your makeup on? What do you mean your mother never taught you how? I didn't really have a mother to raise me and somehow I managed to learn! I have faced the time constraints of motherhood, juggling a career, marriage, and caring for an ailing elderly father. And I know that when something is important to you, you will make time!"

My best friend, Caroline took me out for happy hour, just days before my eldest daughter Marissa's wedding in April 2009. We nursed our Cosmopolitan martinis for nearly three hours. I told Caroline how I wanted to write a new book about beauty, I just didn't know where to begin. Caroline has always been a source of insight and inspiration to me. She is a real get it done kind of woman.

"Oh, that's easy! Just tell your story," she said.

"My story? Which one?" I inquired with a chuckle.

"The one about your life, darling."

"I don't think I can, and I'm afraid no one will find it interesting."
Caroline stared me intently in the eyes and said, "But you must. If you really want to heal this world, you must share your story. Can't you see how it all began and why?"

Then I exhaled a deep breath of relief and let the tears roll down my face. In that moment I was transported back to fifty years ago … back to the beginning. Back to the very first moment I knew that letting one's appearances go was a sign that something was wrong … terribly wrong.

I was very young when the accident occurred, and I could never have grasped the magnitude of it all back then. Amazingly though, I do remember the actual day and I knew that something terrible had happened. My father was sitting with his head buried in his clenched hands. He was sobbing uncontrollably. The house was dark; the only light that shone was when the door opened time and again as friends, neighbors and family members kept coming in and leaving.

One of the few tangible memories I have of my mother is a photo of her and me lying on a blanket at the park. We looked much like any other happy mother and child. Most families have boxes of those kinds of pictures. Mine doesn't, because our time together was so brief, so tragically brief.

My mother was a physically beautiful woman; well dressed, sexy and elegant; a real head-turner I was told. She was a gifted singer with a gorgeous operatic voice. I heard that she had a smile that lit up a room. Marissa, my first born has a smile like that. It's a kind of smile like a ray of sunshine that bursts through a cloudy sky. My father, Nathan, always had a penchant for beautiful women. He and my mom were married about a year before I was born. My beloved father's life was also filled with devastating events, as he endured extreme torment and inexplicable pain as a survivor of the Holocaust. All of his five siblings and their families were killed. So were his parents, grandparents, aunts, and uncles. His young pregnant first wife was killed by the Nazis, as was his three year-old son. Only a few of his cousins and friends lived through the atrocities.

When the Germans invaded Poland, they separated many Jewish families. My father was young and very strong, and the Germans needed men like him to work in their factories. When they tried to take his wife and child, he attempted to fight back with his life. Instead of killing him, they threw him on the ground and beat him into submission with the butt of their gun, damaging his kidney.

In 1950, he came to Los Angeles. His back was still in excruciating pain and he needed to have one of his kidneys removed. He spent over six months recuperating in the original Cedars Sinai Hospital, where his room overlooked the new maternity wing being built. Everyday he stared at the progress and swore to himself that if he lived through this ordeal, someday he would have another child and it would be born in that very building.

On June 12, 1953, in the early hours of the morning, his dream was realized as I arrived in Cedars Sinai's new maternity ward. My dad told me I was so ugly when I was born that he was certain that the doctor made a mistake and gave him the wrong baby! All I did was stick my tongue out at everyone. Perhaps that was an early sign of having my own mind from the start? Maybe, but it took me nearly forty-two years to find that mind! Forty-two years to have my awakening! I'm not complaining. Some women never have an awakening. So to have one at mid-life is a fine thing … Actually, it's a great thing.

So you may be wondering what does all of this have to do with a book about beauty? Everything.

I know that every person has that pivotal moment in their life that changes everything. I call it "their awakening." Mine did not happen during prayer or from a life-threatening circumstance. No, not at all. Mine happened on a hot June day, two days before my 42nd birthday. Neither my host of supportive friends nor angels blowing their trumpets called to wake me up out of my miserable complacency. No, it was my precious little five year-old son, Mitchie who jolted me back to life! I can still remember exactly where we were; funny how those details of life altering moments stay etched in our minds.

I was driving with Mitchie heading north on Kanan Drive in Agoura, California … a lovely suburb in Ventura County. I was stopped at the red light, both hands holding the steering wheel. I even remember I was wearing a blue-gray, long floral sleeveless, baggy, matronly, frumpy, dumpy dress! Got the picture? It was the best of few possible options in my wardrobe at the time.

I wasn't comfortable showing my body anymore because I had gotten so out of shape after the birth of my third child. I almost couldn't recognize myself anymore. I had gone from a rocking fit woman with 17% body fat to an unhealthy 30% body fat! I became a skinny fat person! (Thin at a glance, with the body fat of a heavy person.) Weak, frail and flabby were the unflattering adjectives to describe my body at this time in my life. I also became an expert in denial. As long as I kept all of the other different aspects of my life going, I told myself I was fine.

Actually, I was far from fine. I was falling apart. I was ashamed of my flabby thighs, so no more shorts or short dresses for me! Tight rear-end hugging clothing? Oh, no, not on *my* ass. It had fallen like an undercooked soufflé. My kids called my rear end, "Jell-O-Ass," because it jiggled so much when they playfully slapped it. My lower abdomen, once rock solid, now protruded. And my arms? Well, my arms clapped back when I clapped my hands!

Years of crazy low protein diets, high amounts of stress and lack of exercise weakened and aged my body. I existed on large amounts of caffeine and sweets. My body hurt all of the time. Marissa, who was fifteen years-old at the time begged me to take care of myself. Ha! I had no time for that! I was a working mom in a not-so-happy marriage, with a young child, two teenagers, and a father who had severe Alzheimer's disease. And oh, yeah, I also had an image consulting business and worked about 50–60 hours a week.

"It takes thirty days to form a habit and ninety days to make it yours forever," I say. *"Now let's read our health and fitness commitments. You will need to sign these commitments and keep them in order to honor yourself and improve your life."*

In other words, I was telling my students, "Just do it!" I think I was about 39 or 40 years old when Nike came out with their brilliant ad campaign slogan, "Just Do It."

Oh God, how I hated those ads and the blaringly subtle billboards that haunted me. "What the hell do you mean, Just Do It?" I screamed! "*You do it, damn it! I can't just do it! I have to work, take care of my family, care for my father, be a wife, do community work, cook ... I have a very busy life. Busy moms can't just do it!*"

I would get so angry I would hit the steering wheel as I looked up at the large Nike billboard looming over my car. Sometimes the truth is that the most profound things in life are the most simple. What I desperately needed to do was in fact, "just do it."

Boot camp after boot camp, I listen to the excuses that have kept each of these women from being their best. "*Stop making excuses!! What do you mean you have no time to take care of yourself? What do you mean you have no time to exercise or put on makeup? So you think I've had it easy, huh?*" I demand. "*Let me tell all of you here today that there is almost no excuse you can tell me that I haven't experienced for myself. Almost none!*"

One of the students, who was ready to let go of "her story" (her excuses) tossed the green and black "busted" Nerf ball back to me. I toss this ball as a wake-up call to any woman in the room who thinks I will accept her excuses.

"*Good!*" I shout. "*Now you are ready to move forward.*"

So there we were, Mitchie and I stopped at that red light. I would have been dressed like an Arabic woman in a long black robe and Hijab covering my head and revealing only my eyes if I could have, and not for religious reasons. Instead I was wearing that blue-gray floral dress with my arms bared. Well, it was so damned hot I had to be sleeveless! Out of the blue, my little Mitchie says, "Mommy, what are those things on your arms?" My stomach did a somersault as if I had just gone down a huge rollercoaster ride. "What things, Mitchie?" I replied, fearing the answer.

"Those things, Mommy, those flappies!" Then he reached over and jiggled my upper arms.

I had no reply. I was speechless. Those who know me will attest to the fact that I am rarely ever speechless. Yet there I was, tears streaming down my face as reality knocked me in my head, waking me up out of my self-righteous denial.

"Your body is speaking to you. Listen to it. Pay attention. If you are flabby it's because you need to work out your muscles. Your body is screaming out for help. It's never too late. You're never too old to build muscle mass. Be vain enough to see what your body is telling you!"

I explain the concepts of sarcopenia, the physiology of muscle mass loss. I watch the vacant stares of the women who are in denial. I watch as my words stir something inside of them. I see it in their eyes. I know because I was there.

… A few months before my Mitchie awakening, I attended Governor Pete Wilson's *Call to Action Women's Conference*. There were many break-out sessions. I chose the *Fit For Life* workshop. Maybe because I was quickly becoming unfit for life.

I had the nerve to sit in the front row. Three famous powerful women shared the stage. One was fitness guru, Sheila Cluff, owner of The Oaks at Ojai. Sheila was seventy-two-years-old and a true powerhouse pioneer in the original health and fitness world. Sheila's words rocked me to my core. Sheila spoke about various easy fitness routines for busy working women. Seeing the non-responsive blank stares, Sheila decided to make things easier for us to grasp. She broke it all the way down into three, five minute little exercise routines per day. For a moment or two I thought about how pathetic it was that she needed to cajole women to exercise in five-minute increments. But then, who was I to throw stones? From the look on Sheila's face, I knew she thought it was absurd too. But Sheila was hell bent on making us wake up to the benefits of consistent exercise. So finally Sheila said, "Listen, if you don't want to exercise for yourselves, do it for your family."

Now I really started to squirm in my seat! "Do it for my family?" I thought. What could Sheila mean?

"Do you want to be a burden to your children?" Sheila demanded. "Do you want to use a walker? Be in a convalescent home? Force your children to have to take care of you?"

"Oh, God," I said in my heart. Oh, God! My own father had Alzheimer's, not from lack of exercising his body, but in his case, from lack of exercising his mind, or so I thought at the time! I was haunted by Sheila's words. However, I was the "denial queen" and as such, was reluctant to change my ways. That was, until I had my "Mitchie Moment," as I like to call it.

"Mommy, what are those things on your arms? Those flappies?" I kept hearing my little boy asking me this question over and over again like a bad nightmare. I tried to keep my composure as I choked down the tears and rage. Rage for letting myself fall apart. Rage that even a child could see it. Rage at how out of control my life felt.

After I dropped Mitchie off, I went off to my nail appointment. My manicurist, Monica, was more like a therapist than a manicurist and truthfully, she was better at therapy! She was the slowest manicurist on the planet, so all of her clients talked to her, and talked, and talked, and talked!

Monica asked me why I looked so upset. I quickly told her what my son said and declared to the Universe, "I need a great personal trainer! I need one *now!*"

I am convinced there is truth to the phrase that when the student is ready, the teacher appears. There I was telling Monica how I desperately needed a trainer, and out of the blue she said, "Well then, walk into the next room and tell Arlene that you want to talk to her. She's one of the best trainers around."

"Where? Here in this hair salon? There's a personal trainer here? Why?" I implored.

"Arlene is a part time hairstylist *and* personal trainer. She is really, really good. Go talk to her. Go, go!"

I thought, "How good can this trainer be if she has to work part time in a hair salon?" So I strolled over and peeked around the wall to her station. There before me stood a mature woman wearing a tank top and tight jeans, sporting a rock hard body, strong beautiful sculpted arms and shoulders. The best part was that she looked fantastic! "Sickeningly fantastic," I thought. I knew in my heart, that was a good sign. I took a deep breath and walked up to her.

"Are you Arlene, the personal trainer?" I asked.

"Yes, I am," said Arlene.

"I would like to talk to you about training me. How much do you charge and how long are your sessions? Do you have three evenings a week open for me?"

"Whoa, slow down. Not so fast!" demanded Arlene. "Why do you want to work out?" she asked me.

"Well," I whispered. "I have to wear two pairs of shoulder pads to appear to have shoulders! I am very weak," I replied.

"If I trained you, eventually you wouldn't need any shoulder pads because your shoulders would be naturally strong and defined!" Arlene insisted. That struck my mind like an arrow.

"Really? Sign me up! When can we begin?" I begged.

"Oh, no. Not so fast. I won't train anyone who isn't serious. This is a lifelong commitment. There is no turning back." Next, Arlene asked me two questions I will never ever forget. "I want you to close your eyes. Now imagine that you keep not exercising and eating the way you are now. How will you look and feel in ten years?" Arlene probed.

"Old, feeble and sickly," I whispered ashamedly.

"Now fast forward twenty years ahead," she insisted.

The warm tears streamed down from my closed eyes. "I will be dead!"

"Then walk down another path! Walk down another path," Arlene told me.

"Please, I must do this. You have to help me." I cried.

"No, go home and think about all of this," she said.

"No, I won't leave here without an appointment! I am ready. I must do this, for me and my family." I begged again.

Arlene exhaled, stared me in the eyes and finally said, "I have Mondays, Wednesdays, and Fridays open at 6:30 p.m. See you tomorrow and don't be late. Eat something before. Bring a towel and water."

"You can be Beautiful at any size, any age!" I tell the women at my Beauty Boot Camp.

"Easy for you to say, Eve!" shouts out one of the participants.

"So what are you going to do? Have a pity party? Not like the way you look until you lose the weight and get in shape?" I calmly ask. *"I'll tell you what. You can have a pity party. But then get over putting your beauty on hold. If you start loving the way you look, you will automatically start taking better care of your health."* I admonish.

Pity parties. I was an expert at those. By the time I had reached the age of forty-three, I had become an award-winning expert at having pity parties! I got so good at them, that one day my close friend Susie said, "Eve, enough of these endless pity parties! Okay, I get that you're a victim. Fine. But you need to get on with your life. So, I'll make you a deal. You can have a pity party every Thursday evening from 6:00 to 7:00 p.m. However, if you miss that time slot, you have to wait until the next week to have another one. Okay?" Susie insisted. I had to admit this would force me to stop whining and complaining all of the time … even silently to myself. So I told her, "Fine, I promise. Only on Thursdays from 6:00 to 7:00 p.m."

Guess what? Fast forward a couple of months later and my pity parties were virtually over! What I started to realize is that I could control my life and that no one is a victim, unless he or she believes they are. What on earth possessed me to change this long held point of view? Another friend of mine, Nava, gave me a "tape," a cassette tape to be exact. It was a bad copy of a seminar given by Esther and Jerry Hicks entitled *Abraham*. I leaned over the tape player and strained to listen through the crackling. "Everyone can manifest the life they desire through the power of attraction. By virtue of your thoughts, you can attract to you all that you want." Esther channeled.

"Wait a minute!" I screamed into the empty room. "What the heck do you mean I am not a victim? Gosh damn it, it's not my fault I have an unhappy marriage. It's not my fault I feel like crap. It's not my fault my life is falling apart and that I'm stressed out to the max!" I screamed louder.

"Has everyone here seen or read The Secret? *I know that you are all on a path of self-improvement. How many of you have studied the law of attraction? How many understand vibration and energy flows?"* I ask as I walk over to each table of women. *"Do you realize that your life is evidence of what you have been thinking? Therefore, if you don't like your life, change your thoughts!"* I insist.

For a brief moment I allow myself to remember back to when I was only two and a half, to three years old. I cried and cried that I missed my daddy. "I don't like you," I said to my foster care parents in the midst of one of my many temper tantrums. "I want my daddy. He promised me he would come back. Where is he?" I wept as I looked out of my bedroom window, hoping in vain that my daddy would hear me.

Daddy was busy at work doing everything he could to stay afloat and to support my mom's medical expenses in the hospital. She was never coming out, and the bills never stopped. I couldn't live at home with daddy because he couldn't afford a full time nanny to care for me. The foster home was the only resort. My parents had no health insurance, so my dad worked day and night to try and take care of his family, and the shattered lives we were living. I can't recall much about the foster homes I had to endure for almost three years, except for the beautiful cream, red and black desk and chair set that my daddy bought me for my room. He would visit me once a week and bring me presents. Yes, my very special daddy, I thought as I sucked my thumb and cried myself to sleep each night.

My early childhood is not something I like to talk about anymore. In fact,

I was very reluctant to write about it in this book. I read a few of the chapters to my family, spiritual counselors, and business associates. They all said I must tell the entire story. I said I wanted this book to be about my unique approach to beauty and not about me. I came to realize that one teaches what he needs most to learn. Here we are uncovering, discovering and rethinking the concepts of true beauty.

Through years of self-improvement derived from self-help books, tapes and seminars, coupled with some psychotherapy and a strong determination, I have come to terms with my childhood while learning to nurture the little girl that still lives inside of me. It took years to embrace her, protect her and make her trust again. But as I healed inside, my capacity to understand other women grew. I could feel their pain as I dealt with my own. In a cathartic way, this made sense of the suffering and gave it a purpose that enabled me to have compassion. It also gave me an iron will, determined to help as many women as I could to heal their pain and insecurities. It made me tough enough to stand strongly with other women as they make their own transitions into beauty and wellness. The connection was obvious. At least it was to me.

I now know that God gave me those years to help me become the woman I am today. My inner strength and connection to spirit now serves me well as I help others to improve theirs. I have an unshakeable belief that women need to be elevated into their glory … into the goddess that is inside of each one of them.

"*Yes, you can!*" I affirm loudly. "*Yes, you can have it all. Yes, you are a first class woman. Yes, you can be beautiful, smart and sexy. Yes you can have all of the abundance you want. Yes, you can!*" I even created a special page in their boot camp workbooks entitled *Yes, I Can*. One by one, I ask my students to read a line. It never ceases to amaze me that the line they read is the message they need to hear. God has such a fabulous sense of humor!

In the book, *Conversations With God*, by Neale Donald Walsch, God says, "Well, of course I have a great sense of humor. Who do you think invented humor?"

I love that. I love the entire book.

Truth of the matter is that before my awakening, I would have laughed at that book. I told you about my physical wake up call. But I never mentioned I had a spiritual awakening as well. However, until that time, I didn't dare think of religion any other way than the way my father insisted was the only way …

Judaism. Jews didn't believe that God would talk to an author and co-write a book. God was waiting to bring back the Messiah to the Jews … even if we had to wait until the end of time for it to happen. Jews like my father didn't want to know about self-help. To men like him, self-help meant hard work and determination. It meant saving and investing. Studying was for kids. Adults at that time had no time for that non-sensical luxury. Yet it is precisely the study of God and spirituality that truly changed my life and made me see beauty the way I do today.

In April 2009, I was asked to open the NASDAQ stock exchange, which was an extreme honor and testimony to my belief that beauty is not only important to us personally, but it is essential to global business, and the nation as a whole. My experience of standing at the NASDAQ podium that morning was one of awe and pride. I was humbled and grateful to be invited to greet the world in an arena where President Obama, Oprah Winfrey, and some of the most influential leaders of our country had stood before. This was a sharp contrast to fifteen years earlier when I didn't know how I would live through my second divorce. What I did instead was buy my own home, move my office, and see my oldest child go off to college. Most importantly, I never expected to get past the sadness of my father's death, all which happened within six months! I did live through it and eventually flourished. Now I bless those years. I truly believe that a woman never really falls in love with herself until she finds out what she is made of and finds her inner strength. Then and only then will she know she can survive anything. I am living proof of that.

As I write this, I am sitting in my red and gold meditation room, my beautiful sanctuary of sanity as I like to call it. I am facing a white statue of Quan Yin, the Chinese goddess of love. On the table is the prayer of St. Francis of Assisi, near a hologram of St. Anne de Beaupre, the mother of miracles. She is holding the Holy Mother Mary standing in peaceful repose. On the table and in the cabinet are volumes of metaphysical books. They are my treasures, more than money or gold could ever represent.

"Now let us form a circle, holding hands. Good, gather around. Let's take three deep cleansing breaths. Exhale all of your fears, worries and doubts out of your body. Let go. Breathe in and relax." I slowly begin. *"Thank you Divine Universal Energy for bringing us together in light and love. Thank you for creating this space for us to share and celebrate our beauty. Thank you for helping us to uplift one another.*

For the first time, maybe ever, we will be in a group of women, helping each other to be our best. We agree to keep this time together and what is said between us sacred. Thank you for these three days. I am honored and blessed to guide you on your path to letting your true beauty shine from the inside out. I know this to be true, even now. So Be It and So It Is, Amen," I say, as we loosen our hands and slowly open our eyes.

CHAPTER THREE

Comfort and Style are Not Enemies

"Eve, we love your shoes! They are so beautiful. But how do you wear those high heels? How do you walk in them?" A couple of my new boot camp students ask me on the first day of class …

"I can't wear nice shoes. They hurt my feet." One lady chimes in.

"No one sees me. Why bother trying to wear heels? I wear sweats and Uggs. I work from home. I just need to be comfortable. Heels aren't comfortable," says another participant.

Next thing I knew, everyone is whining about how sexy shoes hurt their feet. My students sign up for my Beauty Boot Camp months in advance. They know it's a makeover workshop and they know it's about image. The fees are high as I want them invested in their transformation and I need them to take this seriously. They have to really want to make a profound positive change in their image, so we have a dress code, as follows: no sweats, no denims, no flip-flops, no logo t-shirts. We send emails well in advance. They know what's expected of them.

I have to tell you that the reaction to this dress code is shocking to me. But after years of teaching my boot camps, I am getting used to it. Invariably we get a few women each class who moan, groan, and even cry to my assistant that they don't own anything other than sweats or denims. They call us all distraught and say that they don't know what to do. My assistant tells them, "Buy a dress or a pair of pants and a nice top. Look in your closet, I'm sure you have something you can pull together."

There we were, the very first morning of class and the participants are settling in after our prayer circle. My eyes take them in and assess where they are in regard to their image skills. I look at their hair and makeup. One beautiful African American woman has no makeup on. Not a stitch. Now to me, not wearing any makeup is like wearing a suit with no shirt. It just doesn't fly. I totally get the natural "fresh" looking makeup. I even get wearing it so it doesn't look like makeup. What I *don't* get is the "just washed my face and ran out the door" look. So I stop and ask this beautiful tall athletic looking woman why she didn't have any makeup on.

"Who me?" she asks.

"*Yes, you!*" I reply. "*Would you go on a first date or a job interview without makeup on?*" I probe.

"Well, makeup takes too much time and besides, I forgot it at home." They can tell from the expression on my face that this isn't going to fly with me.

I ask her, "*What do you mean you forgot it? You travel without makeup?*"

Her eyes well up with tears and she says, "I am a physician, an anesthesiologist. I am married and have three sons. Even my dog is a male. I am surrounded by masculine energy and I have forgotten what it's like to be a feminine woman. As long as I excelled at school and sports, it was enough in my family. My husband sent me to your workshop. He has been begging me to look more feminine; more sexy. I don't know how. I don't know what that even feels like." Then the tears fall down her face.

"*You will learn. All I ask is that you are open to doing things differently, so you can get different results.*"

There are many tears at my boot camp, mostly tears of relief. These women have spent years wanting to learn how to look better with no one to teach them, and nowhere to learn what they needed or wanted to know. Now they have the chance to step into their true beauty and shine. They are overwhelmed. Some are terrified. I remind them to look at the poem again, *Our Greatest Fear*. I smile and ask them to let their lights shine and to give themselves permission. They come to me from all walks of life: physicians, attorneys, psychologists, investors, realtors, stay-at-home mothers, teachers, health practitioners, accountants, pilots, life coaches, ex-military personnel, speakers, beauticians, you name it. Rich and poor; super intelligent and not; every race, every religion, straight or gay, tall or short, all sizes, and all ages. They come to me to learn how to look and feel more beautiful. I will give them the skills they are looking for.

Image is a very emotionally charged subject. Our egos love to play tricks on us and hold us locked in fear. That's why I always ask everyone I work with to leave his or her ego outside in the parking lot. We don't need our egos getting in the way of our progress. You see, our egos tell us that we don't need to change, that we know what to do even when we don't. Our egos fight change, kicking and screaming each step of the way. So egos are banned from my boot camps, along with ugly sweat pants and flip-flops. With the battle of the "ego," there are many new skills to be learned and mastered. There are years of neglect to undo and self-esteems to rebuild. But first, each and every student must understand the importance of having a stylish image and understand why that is more important than comfort or convenience.

"Everyone! Please take out your pen and notebook. Write this down. COMFORT AND STYLE ARE NOT ENEMIES," I shout! No one moves. Their eyes are wide open. *"You are so preoccupied with being 'comfortable'. I'll tell you about my feelings about comfort,"* I begin. *"When I am wearing a beautiful outfit that flatters my body; when I'm dressed in colors that look good on me; when I can walk all day in my gorgeous high heels; when my hair looks great and my makeup is on, and when I turn heads, get the respect I deserve, and love the way I look ... that's when I feel comfortable. Very, very comfortable!"*

My students start smiling. They like my theatrics. They like that I am a colorful speaker. You know what I like? I like how I can see that a light just went off in their beautiful heads. I know that they never thought of comfort this way. They are starting to get how ridiculous our national obsession is with comfort. It would serve us better as a nation to be obsessed with beauty, elegance and style. It's not that I am opposed to comfort. I like comfort as much as the next person. But you don't have to be sloppy or slovenly to be comfortable, and sadly many people have become sloppy in their quest for comfort. What I want to do is redefine comfort in regard to style.

I continue, *"I have spoken with many psychotherapists about my theories. Many of them have told me that when people let their appearance go it is a form of depression. So if you are not depressed, why on earth would you want to look like you are? Why wouldn't you want to present yourselves in the best possible light? I will go one step further. Every day people see you, right? They are looking at you, any time you are in the public, with others. Well, I guarantee you that your appearance will either depress those people looking at you or it will make them feel better! Rest assured, it will have an effect one way or the other. You are the one who gets to decide every day which reaction you will elicit. I choose joy. I want to be a beneficial presence in this* world. I want to let my beauty shine. I want the same for each and every one of you. I want you to be the 'light' that dispels darkness.

"Why on earth would Americans think that comfort and convenience is the best thing in life? While I'm not advocating men wear suits and ties 24/7 or women be enslaved in tight corsets and squeezed into stiff dresses, I am saying that anything worthwhile takes more effort, including how you present yourselves. The way this country is headed with this comfort/convenience/not caring phase, we will soon wear pajamas to work! Why not, they are super comfortable, aren't they? How low can we go?

"Can any of you imagine sending a client your business plan in a coffee stained envelope on torn up stationery, rumpled and crumpled with smeared ink?" I inquire as everyone laughs. "What about going to the bank to make a deposit and your bank teller is unshaven, dirty and wearing a sloppy stained logo t-shirt, shorts and Teva sandals?" I shout. "Would that make you feel good about where you have your money? No, of course not. Well, when you don't care about how you present yourselves, it is equally ridiculous. The negative messages are the same."

A few of the participants raise their hands to ask me a question.

"Eve, okay, I get that we need to pay more attention to how we dress. But are you trying to tell us that you expect us to dress up everyday, all the time?" asks Linda.

Then Beth shouts out, "Yeah, that's what I want to know. I mean no disrespect, but we can't all be like you."

Another student says, "I bet you even dress up to go to the gym!!"

"No, I don't," I say. "But I am always well coordinated, clean, and have just a bit of makeup on. That way, I feel good about myself and I stay true to my essence of being a well-dressed fashionable woman. After the gym I may get coffee or run some quick errands. With a little lip gloss, blush and sunglasses on, worn with stylish work-out clothes, I feel presentable. Besides, we never know who we will run into when we least expect it. I remember a few years ago, I had an audition with the head of programming for Merv Griffin Productions. Of course, I dressed myself as beautifully as I could for this meeting. Then two days later, on Sunday, my husband wanted to go to Costco. I can still hear him asking me why I didn't just throw something on so we could go. 'Honey, it's just Costco,' he said. 'Robert, you never know who you can meet at Costco. I'll be ready soon,'" I said.

"Wow, you look so cute, even though you're casual. Nice job!" Robert complimented.

Off to Costco we go. I am in the meat department, waiting for a rotisserie chicken when all of a sudden I hear a man call out to me, "Eve Michaels? Hi, it's Matt."

"Who?" I asked as I turned around.

"Matt, from Merv Griffin. I'm here shopping with my wife."

"Now, do you think I was glad that I took an extra fifteen minutes to prepare myself that day? You're darn right I was. Otherwise, I would have been mortified. Because in a million years, I would never have expected to meet that man ten miles from my home at Costco that Sunday. Never!"

The moral of this story is that often times the best opportunities of our lives come when we least expect them: we encounter a person who can catapult our career; the man (or woman) of our dreams; the contact we have been trying to get an appointment with. You get the picture.

"This is why we need to package ourselves to communicate the same person 24/7, wherever we go. Yes, because we have to and yes, because we get to. It's an honor and a privilege. That's an important concern that many people have when they begin this journey; if they have to dress up all the time. What I want you to know ... Everyone, write this down! You MUST be the same person 24/7 whether you are dressed for the gym, going to the market, at work, out for dinner, or at a cocktail party/formal. You must communicate who you are and the message must be consistent! People have to 'get you.' You don't have to be dressed up all day, every day. But you must put out effort to look good. Aside from pride, it's a matter of self-respect and self-love."

"What does that mean, '24/7' Eve? I don't get it."

"Yeah, how do you do that at the gym or on a hike? Seriously, how?" everyone asks.

"You put stylish clothing on you that is in your right colors, even if it's workout clothes; you fix your hair and makeup for the occasion (for the gym, maybe a ponytail and a little bit of makeup) and your clothing fits you properly and is flattering. You are well-groomed, clean, and your clothing is in good repair. Your outfit coordinates. You smell good and look presentable," I explain.

"What this really means is that you always take pride in your image. You also take time every single day to prepare yourself to face the world. Whether its fifteen minutes or an hour, you must put thought, planning, and energy into your appearance. Believe me your efforts will be rewarded. We used to know this as a nation.

We used to know this as a people. We used to do this individually. We can't afford not to do this now! More than ever it will be the people who package themselves to their best advantage that will get the job, get the business, and get the promotion. We'll discuss this more when we talk about the Art and Science of Dressing Well. For now, trust me that true comfort comes when you are respected, admired, and do well in life. Your image has a very powerful effect on those around you, if you all only understood the magic at your disposal. If you only understood how your lives could improve just by how you present yourselves, then you would never choose comfort over style. No, instead you would find a way to be comfortably stylish!" I urge.

"You see, even pajamas or a nighty can be beautiful and comfortable for bed. Does it take more thought, more effort to find stylish clothing that is also comfortable? Yes, a bit more. But soon after graduating from this course, you will find doing this easier and easier. You will understand the method and you'll find shopping to be a joy, rather than an exercise in frustration."

My mind begins an inner dialogue "Eve calm down. That's why they're here, to learn from you. But these are professional women for goodness sakes! What on earth are they thinking? They're *not* thinking! They never learned the importance of looking good. Oh, this is a tough group. But I'll get through to them." I always do. The hardest thing for me to understand is why people of means in this country, who have a good education and are intelligent, don't understand the importance of taking pride in their appearance. For much of the world, looking good is a given … something you do everyday like showering and brushing your teeth.

"It sounds like most of you are very concerned with comfort when you dress. You want comfort, cheap and easy. However on the other hand, you all want to earn more money, have more confidence and higher self-esteem. You take thousands of dollars a year in self-improvement seminars. You read the 'how to' books and say your affirmations. Yet, every time you look in the mirror you see the same person you were before; no changes, no improvements. So how do you really know you have changed? More importantly, how does anyone else?"

I continue, "What I really want to know is why do we, as a nation, think if someone is stylish that they won't be comfortable? For generations, the upper class, wealthy people have known that the best, most luxurious fabrics are very comfortable. There is no comparison for example between Chinese cashmere and Italian cashmere. Egyptian cotton is one of the finest and softest cottons in the world. Calfskin leather is the *supplest leather and the lightest. Do you get my point? Luxury and elegance can be very comfortable! Think about it. Luxury cars have always been the most comfortable and the best to drive. Down pillows are better than foam. The higher thread count sheets are the softest and also the most expensive. Again, do you get my point? If you can afford these things, then go for it. If you can't, then find a way to buy the best things you can. You can buy at resale consignment stores, discount stores, and on-line stores. Where there's a will, there's a way. When you have a choice, always choose quality over quantity ... as it will speak volumes about you and serve you well.*

"Our issues with food are the same. We opt for quantity over quality, because most people don't even know what real, organic, farm fresh produce tastes like. Our taste buds have been tricked into liking chemical ridden processed foods that have too much salt, sugar, and transfats in them. What's worse is that we have been brainwashed to expect our food to last for weeks or months instead of days. Why? Convenience.

"Then we become overweight or obese. We get sick. We get cancer and auto-immune diseases. Let me tell you clearly, that is NOT comfortable or convenient!! Taking the apparent 'easy way out' usually is not. Laziness never yields great results except on a rare occasion.

"The good news is that we can change this mindset with effort and awareness. Ever so slowly, I see the tides are beginning to turn. Slowly, we are beginning to wake up to the idea that 'less is more' and 'quality lasts.'

"Some old fashioned values are healthy for us. Beauty and style are not solely meant for a party or a special occasion. Our lives are not programs we can put 'on hold.' Our lives are meant to be lived to the fullest, and the beauty within us needs to be expressed every single day.

"This concept is something Hispanics know. It is something African Americans know. It is something Europeans know. They know (and have known) that the quickest way to be perceived as successful is to look like you are. We can learn from them. Caucasian Americans, in my opinion, have become too complacent over the last thirty years. And that makes me nervous! That also makes me and a lot of other Americans, very uncomfortable! The rest of the world doesn't care about comfort; they care more about succeeding, being well-educated, and getting the respect they deserve. Much of the rest of the world is also starting to surpass us in education, productivity, and economic growth."

CHAPTER FOUR

The Five Stages of Grieving

I ask the students to take their seats and open their workbooks. I take a deep breath as I begin teaching the concepts of change and The Five Stages of Grieving as I call them, based on the teachings of Elizabeth Kubler-Ross (The Five Stages of Grief). Teaching this part of my workshop is vital to my students' success as I help them see that even a change of identity/new image can trigger the feelings associated with the grieving process.

Today, I am teaching one of my Image and Beauty Boot Camps for Women. Last week, it was The Men's Overhaul Program. The subject matter is largely the same; the science of image is universal, but the art of it is more gender specific. The actual difference is in how the two sexes learn this subject matter. The men want to be convinced as to why they should change their image: how it will help them earn more money, get more respect, and improve their love lives. Women want to feel beautiful: to learn every detail, every nuance, and then apply the information in a very personal way. Men want to learn: get the wardrobe and get out. Women want to be nurtured through the process and take their time. Women usually don't want the workshop to end. I can't help but smile.

I stand in the center of the room. *"I would imagine that by now your heads are spinning from all of the information you have learned this morning. I'm also certain that you are all experiencing many mixed emotions; elated one moment, upset and depressed the next. This is very normal. We have so many emotions, both negative and positive attached to our appearance,"* I carefully say. *"We also have them attached to change, which is very challenging for most of us. You may be thinking things like, 'My image is fine. I don't even know why I'm at this workshop!' Maybe you're thinking, 'This is ridiculous! Looking better won't help me earn more money or have the relationship of my dreams!'*

"You may not believe this, but I understand you more than you know. I have felt what you are feeling … many, many times," I tell them.

For a moment I am back in that luxury car with my celebrity client's father and mother driving around Beverly Hills. Years earlier I began working with and wardrobing a well known movie star and was quickly enlisted by his family to do the same for them. That day I was working on the dad's wardrobe. He was the driver and his wife was in the front seat. I remember that I was sitting in the back as he drove us to another clothing store. I can still hear him lecturing me about what men find attractive. I was going through my second divorce. I had worked out hard to have a nice body again (after my "awakening") … and I was actually in the best shape of my life. Yet, I still dressed in baggy "appropriate" clothing: showing no cleavage, wearing nothing too short and definitely nothing too tight! My soon-to-be ex didn't like me to wear sexy clothing. I was lost in my thoughts, preoccupied with the wardrobe I was creating for my client when all of a sudden I heard him talking to me, bringing my mind back to the present moment.

"Eve, are you listening to me?" He asked loudly. "Look at that girl crossing the street. She looks fantastic in that short skirt and heels!" I thought, I don't wear short skirts.

I said, "Doesn't that look slutty?"

"No! That looks sexy. Big difference," he replied. "Oh, look at that woman over there! Look at her tight fitted dress. Amazing! Notice how she's showing off her figure. Wow!" he said with excitement.

On and on he went, block after block. He talked, he pointed out the well-dressed women and I listened. My neck strained to see everyone he pointed out. I was trying to take in every nuance. The ironic thing was that his wife was sitting beside him in the front passenger seat. She was a large sized woman. But she liked to show off her full figure. I loved her confidence! I, on the other hand was a size four, and only wore conservatively chic (and matronly) clothing! My fashion sense had been influenced by eight years of marriage to a man who liked me to dress "properly," (Properly, a.k.a. a matronly frump.) He loved to look at sexy women and girly magazines, but he definitely didn't want any other man to look at his wife "that way." I've come to find that many men think like that, but thank goodness, not all.

There I was, snapped out of my reverie again by my newfound fashion guru who was hell bent on having me see the light.

"My goodness! Woman! Pay attention! This is important!" he implored as I zoned out, staring into space. "You are going to want to date again, right? Well, you have to understand how we men think! If we aren't attracted to a woman physically, then we don't want to date her. Get it?" He almost shouted. Poor guy was having a hard time getting through to me.

Then I had the audacity to say one of the dumbest things I've ever said. "I want a man who loves my soul first and foremost; a man who loves the inside of me; who I am as a person."

To which he replied, "Babydoll, if a man doesn't want to have sex with you, he won't take the time to get to know your soul or your personality! First, you show off something: your cleavage, your waistline, your booty, or your legs … at least one area. Second, you make sure you look classy. Third, you wear sexy high heels. Fourth, you walk like you love being a woman! Trust me, you'll have more men than you can handle! The best part is that once a guy 'wants' you, he'll take the time to know you and your soul."

"He will?" I leaned over and asked.

"Yes, he will, if he's the right guy," he assured me. "It's your job to take what I've taught you, change the way you dress, and attract Mr. Right."

There was no use arguing. I knew that this very handsome, very educated, very famous man was right. Other friends had tried to tell me similar messages over the years, but I let myself fall into the "my husband likes me like this" trap. My angels must have been watching over me. Either that or Cupid was convinced he could never use his arrow on me until I had the "sexy makeover." It didn't matter. All that counted was that I heard the message loud and clear. That was a life changing car tour; an epiphany!

I was excited and dying to try this new look. I was scared too. Actually, very scared. I had almost forgotten who the sexy Eve was. After all, I reasoned, how could I be a great image consultant, if I didn't know how to dress women in sexy clothing? What was I thinking? All work, no play? I vowed it was time for me to expand my horizons and learn all about dressing sexy, for me and for my clients! Time for Evie to come out of her cocoon. My present husband finds this story unfathomable, knowing me as he does. He just can't understand how I was a good image consultant if I didn't know how to dress people, women in particular, in a way that brought out their sexiness, especially for social occasions. What he doesn't realize is that back then I mostly did corporate work and for that, I didn't need to know much about sex appeal … or so I thought. Obviously, I just didn't know better. So … first stop was Sara's Lingerie.

My fashion guru/driver and expert on "how to get your sexy on" client's wife had introduced me to Sara's.

She said, "Eve, I need to get some smoothing bras and panties. Let's stop by Sara's. She has the best lingerie selection in all of Los Angeles and she can fit large women!" I was embarrassed to say I had never been to Sara's, but I confessed and walked into a wondrous new world of possibilities.

Sara's Lingerie turned my world upside down! I had never seen so many breathtakingly gorgeous bras, panties, negligees, garters; you name it. They were all made in Europe from the finest lace, silks and cottons. This was a lingerie paradise; an elegant, fine lingerie paradise for the smallest woman, size zero to a plus size twenty-six! The endless array of fabrics and colors almost took my breath away. I was intoxicated by the sensuality that filled the room and my mind. I often tell my boot camp students that Sara's helped get me divorced and her lingerie helped get me remarried!

I will never forget I took my husband (number two) to Sara's to buy me a Valentine's Day present. All he could do was bitch about the price, saying those expensive panties would only last six months. He was furious that I wanted to spend so much money on those "things." Embarrassed and disgusted by his behavior, I told Sara to hold all of the pieces I liked, vowing that I would be back. The very next day I went there and bought three bras with matching panties, a robe, and a nightgown. I felt victorious and powerful. I couldn't wait to wear my new lingerie.

I knew my ex would be angry that I spent so much on lingerie without his approval. But I was convinced that once he saw me in the bras and panties, he would be so turned on that he wouldn't mind the hefty price. My girlfriends had told me that men love sexy lingerie so much that they forget about the price tag when their woman comes out dressed to thrill. So I was certain that my hubby would change his mind. I paid Sara with a check from my own business account. I thought it would be a kind of "win-win", if you know what I mean.

For the "unveiling" I waited until the kids were asleep and my husband was in bed watching TV. I went into the closet and put on the white lace very low cut push up bra and matching thong panties with the little peephole and tiny bow on the rear. I was delighted with how I looked in this lingerie … my first expensive elegant lingerie ever! I took a deep breath, walked in front of the TV set and struck a sexy pose. Then I slowly turned around so he could see my backside. Silence! Just silence.

So I finally turned back around and looked at him quizzically and said, "Well, what do you think?"

To my utter amazement, he replied, "Doesn't that thing hurt your ass? Isn't it uncomfortable 'up in there'?"

Well, you could have knocked me over with a feather! Obviously this wasn't the response I had been waiting for! At that moment I vowed that I would never, ever marry another man who didn't appreciate sexy beautiful lingerie. I made that vow because I knew our rocky marriage was close to an end. Then I took off the goods, put on a frumpy pair of pajamas and went to sleep.

We did end up getting a divorce. So, fast forward seven years later, when I met my present husband, Robert. I had just moved into a luxury apartment complex in Beverly Hills after selling my last home. I remember I was so upset at having to rent an apartment, albeit a luxury one after years of owning my own home. But my good friend Ana told me that the Old Testament says, "Change your home; change your luck!" Allison, Robert's daughter was the leasing agent there, and we became friends. For almost three months she tried to get us to meet. Now that is what I call tenacity! I'll never forget the day she called me to meet him at a coffee shop in Beverly Hills. I was out running errands and had no time to go home first. But you know me, always dressed for success! On that Saturday, I was dressed for "being attractive to men" success (which had now become the norm for me.) At 5:25 p.m. I walked in to meet Allison and her dad. I still remember what I was wearing, so does Robert. I had on a white stretchy lace blouse, boot cut denims, and black lacey ankle boots. Underneath peeking out of the lace blouse was that gorgeous white low cut lace push up bra that had turned my ex's nose up seven years ago!

As memory serves, it wasn't a warm day, only 72 degrees outside and air-conditioned inside. But after I sat down with them and we began talking, Robert started to sweat from his face more than any person I had ever seen. He looked like someone had poured an entire bottle of water on his head. I assumed that he had that over-active sweat gland disease called hyperhydrosis! "Poor guy, how would I ever kiss him?" I thought to myself. "My make-up would run right off my face from his perspiration!"

What I didn't realize at the time was that Robert was taken back by my gorgeous European bra, which he knew was a sign of classiness and sensuality. Robert had spent most of his career traveling to Europe where sexy lingerie was and still is the norm. But he had met very few American women who knew about the importance of wearing it. Men are so visual! If only more women understood just how much!

Years later Robert confessed that the combination of that lingerie, my personality, intellect, and the way I presented myself totally took him by surprise! When I asked him if he had ever perspired like that when he met someone, he said he had not. Not even when he met President Reagan at The White House to be part of his first defense trade mission to China, nor when he gave speeches to the chairmen of boards of major corporations. Never! Now I am not so egotistical to tell you that I am all that and a bag of chips! But I did know how to package myself in a way that appealed to men with class.

We were married five months later. I have been buying and happily wearing Sara's lingerie every day ever since. Oh, and that famous white bra and panties that my ex said would only last six months? They lasted over ten years, helped bring my sexy back and attract a wonderful husband. Now that's value, wouldn't you say?

By now you must be wondering what all of this has to do with change? Everything, you see. I listened to my client about the importance of being sexy. I took his lesson to heart. Then I did something about it because I realized I needed to change. That in turn helped me date much more easily. My confidence as a woman soared. Then I met the love of my life, Robert, who wouldn't have been so smitten with me if I hadn't made that important decision to step into my sexiness. Now after nine years of marriage, we continue evolving and changing… together! We know that keeps us fresh, modern and young-at-heart. We embrace change in all of its painful, joyful aspects. And he still loves me to wear beautiful classy lingerie. Thank goodness some things never change!

"You see, even the most positive change is painful! Yes, write that down in your notebooks. Even the most positive change is painful," I say while I look into all of my students' eyes. *"Most of us are afraid to change. Our loved ones don't like us to change. Heck, often times, they don't like us to get a new hairdo, let alone a new image. Even if the old one doesn't serve us, our family and friends are usually the last people to acknowledge that we need to evolve. They feel comfortable with how*

we look, even if our image doesn't serve us any longer. Jealousy may even be a motivating factor. Perhaps they worry that we may look TOO good. They still behave as if there's some unspoken comfort in sameness. But truthfully, there are only two things we can do: change or stagnate, because nothing in this world stays the same. It is either growing and changing or stagnating and dying. Therefore, one could say, that 'life is change.' And so, I choose change over stagnation any day of the week. Now, instead of seeing change as frightening, I can see it as an exciting adventure.

"Sometimes we instigate the change and sometimes the change comes uninvited. We never know what's in store. We as Americans have always been pioneers for change. From equal rights to technology, medical advances to the space program and beyond. Yet on a personal level, we often tend to fight change and this doesn't serve us. Without sounding trite, change is the momentum that propels us forward through the adventures in life. The only constant is that nothing stays constant, especially not in this fast paced, high technology, new world we live in! If you don't change, you're in big trouble," I say with all seriousness. "The biggest lesson of this decade is to embrace the newness, move forward with it, and learn how to use it to your advantage. Wouldn't you all agree?"

Many years ago, about seventeen to be precise, I was working with a client who had her PhD in adult education. Sue came to me because after speaking one afternoon to a group of college students, one of the male students came up to her and said, "You know Doctor, when I first saw you I thought, 'What can this old woman teach me that I would be interested in?' I mean you look so out of touch. But as I listened to your lecture, I was really impressed with what you had to say. Thanks."

Doctor Sue was devastated. It was her "come to Jesus", aha moment to say the least! Once she stopped reeling from her student's brutal honesty, she recognized that her image was interfering with her message. Being a very intelligent woman, she came to realize that not too many students would pay serious attention to her lectures if they were so turned off by her outmoded appearance. Once she understood that her image needed a turn around, she hunted for an image consultant to help her achieve her goals. She ended up being one of my best students because of her desire and ability to learn. Sue quickly changed her image and learned to look fresh, modern and competent, all of which would serve her well. She went from looking highly unremarkable and matronly to looking twenty years younger and fabulous in one month!

I came to deeply respect Sue and her professional acumen. So after we worked together for a while, I offered her a sort of business proposal. I wanted Sue to help me expand my concepts about image making and assist me in developing a questionnaire for my new clients, so that I could be more effective with them. I explained that I have always had a penchant for psychology and a hunger to understand what motivates people to change (or not.) Sue was eager to help me and we decided that we would exchange her time for my time. In other words, we would trade image consulting for educational psychology.

One day, when Sue was in my office reviewing my questionnaire, an idea came to me. For a while I was wondering why people get so upset when they realize that they need to make a significant change in their lives, to a point where it almost seems like they're grieving. Then I started to realize that every time I know that a major fashion/trend is happening, I would get upset and grieve. I would grieve the fact that I liked the fashions, that I knew how to wear them and I didn't want to have to learn an entire "new look" again, let alone have to buy it, integrate it into my wardrobe and then teach about it. Not when I was so busy! I started to do research at the library. (Yes, we used to go to libraries to do research twenty years ago. After all, I've been at this for a long time!) At the library it dawned on me that going through an image change is identical to going through the grieving process or what's more aptly known as Kubler-Ross' Five Stages of Grief. I couldn't wait to tell Sue about my theory and get her input.

I can still remember the look of excitement on Sue's face as I eagerly shared my revelations with her. Sue thought my premise was brilliant and right on point! I wanted to incorporate teaching the stages of grieving into my seminars, workshops and private consultation work. I wanted to create an easier environment for profound and lasting change. Soon after that meeting, I created my new detailed Image Intensive Questionnaire and also began putting The Five Stages of Grieving (my spin on the Five Stages of Grief) into my workbooks and began using the concepts in all of my teachings. It has helped thousands of people to change with greater joy, ease, and understanding. And truthfully, it has also helped me facilitate more lasting change, much more quickly than ever before.

"I can see that most of you are pretty uncomfortable at this point. I can see many emotions bubbling under the surface waiting to come out. You look overwhelmed and anxious," I say with great empathy. *"Let's talk about these feelings. Have any of you*

heard about The Five Stages of Grief *by Kubler-Ross?"* I ask as I look around the room.

A few of my students raise their hands. "Eve, do you mean like when someone dies?"

Another student says, "When my mother died, the therapist talked about the different stages of grief. It was helpful."

The energy in the room just turned on like a bunch of light bulbs! I grabbed my magic marker and walked over to the flip chart. *"Let's talk about the significance of each phase of the grieving process and how it relates to your makeover,"* I say carefully.

"Denial! The first stage is denial," One of the women shouts.

"D-e-n-i-a-l." I look over my shoulder and say, *"Ah ha, that's right. Denial. That's a big one. I can see that many of you are thinking, 'Oh, Eve can't mean me. My image isn't that bad. I make okay money. My husband (or partner) loves me. My sex life is pretty good (well maybe not that good.) I don't see the need to waste money and time to improve. What does she know anyway?'"*

I continue talking as I walk to each table. *"I understand that this is the toughest part of the grieving process. When change is thrown at us, it's easier to deny the need to change than to admit that we need it. Men are masters at denial when it comes to changing their image. In fact, in my experience, men stay stuck a lot longer in this phase. I usually have to work very hard to convince them why they should listen to me and take any of my advice,"* I say emphatically. *"We women are used to hearing criticism from others and, the constant criticism we tell ourselves. We are used to working on our issues or at least acknowledging that we need to improve. Men on the other hand have more of a 'if it ain't broken, don't fix it' kind of attitude. That's why we see older men wearing the same hairstyle since high school or college. They think it is fine!"* Everyone in the room laughs and agrees. *"However there is a huge difference between fine and great; A big gap in perception and execution, wouldn't you say?"*

I started to reminisce about a man named Norm who attended my Men's Overhaul Program in New York a couple of years ago. Norm heard me speak at a huge event he had attended with his business partner, who dressed very well and cared about the importance of having a great image. He actually insisted that Norm sign up for my program. Norm was a little insulted because he felt he had always been successful in business. His business partner was convinced

Norm could be far more successful if he looked the part; modern, manicured and polished.

Norm was tough. Nice, highly intelligent, but very tough. It took all of my expertise and motivational skills to get him out of the stage of denial to begin to transform his image. But Norm didn't think he really needed my help. Most people think that image is optional, especially men. They believe that if they are successful, that is somehow enough … So they wear the same hairstyles and outdated clothes they have since college. They think clothing is something to cover their bodies and to be purchased once or twice a year with much haste and little thought. They have convinced themselves that looks don't matter. Intelligence and tenacity are what counts to men like Norm. He refused to go through the grieving process. He went along with the makeover, but with an attitude of, "I'm just doing this to placate you and my associate. This isn't going to do me any good. This is a ridiculous waste of my time."

On the final day we went shopping, I literally had to force Norm to open his wallet and buy a new mini-wardrobe. Oh, he fought me on every item. Then Norm went home with his new hairstyle, whitened teeth, modern conservative wardrobe, and miracles started to happen! Norm subsequently wrote me two or three emails telling me that he wished he had known about the power of image years earlier. He never realized how much easier doors would have opened for him in business if he had looked better. I guess, Norm didn't move into acceptance until his makeover was complete and he went back to his regular life. Only then could he see and feel the difference it made, in terms of how he was perceived and received. It took him that long to get through the five stages of grief. The important thing is to get to acceptance, and be grateful that you were able to evolve and change.

The women giggle nervously as I obviously struck a chord. Changing one's self willingly is difficult and very rare.

"Let's move on. What's the next phase?" I ask everyone.

Someone jumps up and says, "A-n-g-e-r!!"

"Yes. Anger," I repeat. "Ohhh, yes, I can feel the anger oozing out of many of you here today. I can almost hear you saying, 'What the hell does Eve understand? It's easy for her to look good. After all, money has always been handed to her. She shops all the time. She doesn't know what it means to be on a budget or struggle. Ms. Beverly Hills has had an easy life! She can't relate.'

"If you all only knew. I have been faced with almost every challenge you have. And truthfully, it hasn't always been easy for me to change. I mean...just look at my 'before' pictures! Changing out of that was like climbing my way out of a spiritual, emotional and physical hole, but I knew I had no choice. I literally had to change or die. I chose life and I chose beauty. I have never regretted my choice to change. Never."

"What's the third phase?" I ask.

"Oh, D-e-p-r-e-s-s-i-o-n. Yeah, that's it," says another student, as I write the word down on the flip chart.

I turn around and sigh. "Oh, yes, by now many of you are feeling depressed. I can see you slumping in your seats. Many of you are looking down. You feel badly, for letting your image get neglected, for not making yourselves a priority. But mostly, you feel sad because you feel overwhelmed. You realize how much you have to change and you don't know how you will ever have the time, the money or the skills to continue your makeover."

I lower my voice and whisper, "The truth is that depression is anger turned inward. You are upset with yourselves for getting to this point, but it's great that you are feeling depressed because that means you are on your way to ... next stage?" I ask again.

"The next stage is B-a-r-g-a-i-n-i-n-g, Thank you," I say as I write each answer on the flip chart to emphasize its importance. "Bargaining. You are now a little excited. Your minds are racing. You're beginning to think of solutions instead of problems. You realize that at the minimum you could buy a new lipstick, select one or two pieces of clothing, or try wearing heels. You could see how you look in a different hairstyle. You could have some of your clothing tailored," I say enthusiastically. "Yes! You are starting to actually look forward to this process. The hardest parts are now behind you all. And the last phase? Can someone tell me? It's called A-c-c-e-p-t-a-n-c-e. Congratulations! Most of you are now ready to put forth the time, money and effort needed to transform your appearance. I can see the wheels beginning to turn in your heads. I can sense the feeling of anticipation as you get an idea of how much better you will look and then feel from improving your image! I am so proud of you! Now we are ready to begin," I say with tremendous enthusiasm.

"It's extremely important that you understand that the only difference between you and me is that I have learned to go through the grieving process quicker. In fact every time there is a major fashion change, I feel upset. I go through the five stages of grieving. Just when things get easy, they up and change again. Damn! And there I *go again, having to digest it all quickly so I can help others understand the new trend, the style that's evading them or the hang-ups they're having with their image. I understand that we need to allow ourselves to feel all of the stages and then let them go. Only then can change, true change happen. I have always believed that knowledge will set us free…that includes the knowledge of how we each process, what our stumbling blocks are and what we are afraid of. Many of you here are afraid to look foolish. You're afraid that you won't be able to learn how to keep this beauty going in your lives. You're even afraid that people will think you are vain or worse, that you are trying to look like your teenage children.*

"My spiritual counselor, Trish Loar, tells me that love is an irresistible force. I agree; however, so is beauty. We create beauty because we know on a soul level that it is a powerful healing energy … And energy, as Einstein proved, cannot be created or destroyed. It can only change forms. That is why you are here. You are here to learn how to change forms or better said, to 'transform.' If you allow your greater beauty to be expressed it will gather momentum, transform and heal; it will never die. That is why I teach this and that is why you are here. To express the beauty in you for the entire world to see. Maybe more importantly in the beginning, for you to see!" I tell my students, many of whom have tears in their eyes.

While I was in the process of writing this chapter, our beloved little dog, Mr. Big, died suddenly. He was the love of my husband's life and mine. Our children also adored him. Mr. Big was the picture of health and energy. We gave him such exquisite loving care, we were certain he would live a very, very long life. Then, in exactly two minutes, he went from being an active dog with a seemingly minor paw injury, to dying and leaving us with broken hearts and a house full of memories. I was devastated and angry! I cried harder than I could remember ever crying and so did Robert. We didn't want to be without him. We didn't want our lives to change without notice. This unexpected death shook me terribly.

At this time, I am in the middle of renovating and decorating our very first home in Austin, Texas. We moved here with Mr. Big seven months ago. He was supposed to live with us in our new house. I have been pouring every ounce of my creativity (with our interior designer, Melissa) into making this a home of incredible beauty and comfort. A home that is artistic and uplifting throughout; a home where family and friends adore being, and don't want to leave.

Since Mr. Big passed, I have been frightened that someone or something else I love very much will also leave me. It has bothered me so much that I recently talked about it during my session with Trish. I told her about my fears…fears that I hadn't felt since I was very young. I told her I was afraid for pouring so much love into this new home, for fear it would be taken away from me. I was afraid of another jolting change to my life. It doesn't make logical sense for me to have these fears, but when are fears or grieving ever logical?

All of a sudden, after Trish processed what I had shared with her, she said, "Eve, you have always made every home you have lived in beautiful, that's what you do and how you have chosen to live. The beauty you are creating now will live on in that home long after you no longer live there because beauty is an energy that you create and time will not destroy it … it will be there for the next people who occupy your home someday, and then you will move on and make some place else beautiful."

And so after the initial shock of losing Mr. Big wore off, I started to push myself through the grieving process. I felt my denial, my anger, my depression, and then I bargained, to finally bring myself to acceptance; the acceptance that when things have to change, they have to change. It is not always our job to know or to understand why they have to change. It is our job to find the lesson, the light at the end of the tunnel and the good that comes out of the change.

In a strange and unexpected way, I find that perhaps a newer and greater bond between Robert and me exists since the passing of Mr. Big. Now, instead of turning for comfort to our furry little friend, we spend that extra time connected to one another for those extra minutes of cuddling and affection. As a couple, we never knew we could love something so deeply, and we relish that memory. Now that the void of Mr. Big has subsided just a bit, we are turning that deep love back to each other and we realize that all things happen for a reason. We are choosing to make the best out of this change in our lives, although it is not easy to be at peace knowing everything happens for a reason.

"Maybe comparing losing a loved one to changing one's image seems ludicrous and possibly even rude to you all. I promise you, change is inevitable and that even the most positive change can be painful. Just as stepping out of the darkness into the light can jolt your vision and blind you temporarily. You reach for the light, nonetheless."

I have always told people that I push my students through the grieving process until they see the light…until I see that light turn on in their heads. I always know the moment it happens, because I can feel the release of energy as I watch their energy soar. Once their light is turned on, they will never be the same or look at image the same way again. They have been transformed. I look at my students with great love in my eyes.

CHAPTER FIVE

A Great Image is a Way of Life!

The other day, I came across this quote in an Austin newspaper from a successful hair stylist, Ricky Hodge. Ricky has always believed in the power of image and dressing well, ever since he was a young student in cosmetology school. Clients coming into the school thought he was an instructor, although he was a "newbie," because of the way he dressed and presented himself. When interviewed, Ricky said, 'It's a matter of perception—how you look, how you carry yourself, how you present yourself. When people meet you, it's like when they meet a doctor. You have to be the person who's in their mind." I totally agree. We have to be the person they are expecting or we are sure to make a negative impression.

Think of it this way. A doctor should look like a doctor: educated, elegant, up-to-date, and healthy. A lawyer should look like a lawyer: very successful, detail oriented, and smart. An entertainer should look like he belongs on a stage with all eyes on him. A publicist should look very "in the now and in the know," successful and savvy. I could go on and on, but you get the point. We need to look, for the most part, the way people expect someone in our profession to look. Expectations are extremely powerful and hazardous when not met.

I ask everyone, "*What is a negative impression anyway?*"

Linda says, "Looking bad."

"Well, not exactly, but thank you," I reply. "Anyone else know?"

"Dressing sloppy and out of style", says another student.

"*Again, very valid. However, a negative impression is one that either turns people off to you or your message; stops them from wanting to work with you or get to know you better, or from trusting you and your expertise. It's negative because it does you harm. It also lowers the other person's vibration with the energy of distrust or dislike. Either way or for whatever reason, it's not a good thing.*"

A negative first impression is the worst. Image studies have shown that if we make a negative first impression, it takes about 45 minutes of fancy talking to undo the damage. Now you tell me, who in this fast paced world, will give you 45 minutes of their time for you to undo a negative first impression? We don't get "do-overs" in the adult world, especially not in business. Therefore, it's vital that we know what impression we need to make and IF in fact we are making it at all, every single day. As my very intelligent son-in-law, Avi, says, "It's got to be on point!" Yes, it does … very on point!!

When is your image good enough? When is it on point? The answer is when people easily get who you are; when you don't feel resistance to you or your ideas; when you are received in a way that you want to be received or better; when you are respected for your professional expertise; when doors open wide for you instead of close in your face; when you love the way you look; when who you are on the inside shines through on the outside; and when your image helps you achieve your goals by working for you, not against you. Sadly, many people's image works against them and they don't even know it.

Think about it. Would you babble and blurt out everything that is in your head without giving some thought as to how it will sound to the other person? No, of course not! Why not? Because you know that you have to form your sentences a certain way, select the right words, and use the right timing in order for your communication to be effective. The same rules apply to your image. You can't just put clothes on for the mere purpose of covering your naked body and protecting yourself from the elements. That is pre-historic and archaic. You must do so much more than that in this modern world. Dressing well is both an art and a science. and as with any art, it takes practice. The art and science of dressing well is something that must be learned. In order to execute the art, we must first understand the science. What I have been talking about thus far is the science.

Over fifteen years ago, I took some high-level image certification courses from Angie Michaels (same last name; no relation.) She was the instructor who introduced me to the scientific studies about image in her course, Image Matters. She taught us that all first impressions are based on three components: appearance and actions (body language), voice, and words.

Appearance and body language = 55%; Voice = 38%; Words = 7%

Our voice has little to do with our image unless it is whiney, harsh, or distracting. Our words barely enter into the equation if they are consistent with our message. Good posture conveys a sense of dignity and optimism, or it can give an indifferent or apologetic appearance. Body language only counts if it is distracting or annoying. Body language can help bolster a great image through a confident handshake, by looking people in the eye, by walking tall and holding oneself with an air of healthy self-esteem. With that in mind, simply stated our image can be broken down into two parts:

Appearance (your look) and **Actions** (your body language)

Angie said that the well-dressed person wears clothes that:
- Compliment his/her physical characteristics
- Coordinate in color, fabric, and pattern
- Fit properly
- Are appropriate for the occasion
- Are current

Angie also taught: Your appearance sends signals to others about who you are, how you feel, and gives a sense of your values and aspirations. Looking our best makes us feel better and function better. It also shows respect for those around us.

The Positive Cycle of Success: An **improved image** creates more **confidence,** which helps **improve one's performance,** which gets us **more recognition from peers and others,** which then **raises our self-esteem.**

During that portion of my advanced image training, I found a book by William Thourlby entitled *You Are What You Wear*. After twenty five years of research, Thourlby (an image consultant) came up with a list of the Top Ten Decisions People Make in 30 Seconds or Less, based on our appearance. I have been showing this chart to every student and client for the last eighteen years. Thourlby said when people meet you they determine the following within 30 seconds or less:
- Your economic level
- Your educational level
- Your trustworthiness
- Your social position

- Your level of sophistication
- Your economic heritage
- Your social heritage
- Your educational heritage
- Your success
- Your moral character

"Wow!! All of that in 30 seconds or less? That's not fair!"

"People shouldn't judge us by how we look!"

"If someone dresses nicely, that doesn't mean he or she is a good honest person."

"This is ridiculous."

"I can't believe that my image can tell people my social heritage or my moral character!" My students rant until I calm the group down.

"Listen up! I didn't make the rules, but I sure know how to play by them. Life is not always fair. People should like us for who we are. Everyone should give us a chance. But life is too hectic and there is too much competition for that to ever happen. You'd be better off acknowledging the reality of what your image is saying, good or bad. Do something to make it right. Isn't that why you are here?" I knew by their faces, it was.

Yes, our sense of sight directly affects how we feel. It is like there is a beeline from our eyes straight to our gut (our solar plexus.) Isn't that why we love beauty in all forms? Architecture, music, design, food presentation, gifts, gardens, you name it. We love being surrounded by beauty. Beauty makes us feel better. No one can deny that.

Now let's talk about the interviewing process. When a person applies for a new job, he/she sends out his/her resume. If the HR person likes your resume, he will ask to meet you in person. Why? So they can see how they feel about you! I can guarantee you if they don't like what they see, you won't get hired. The message you communicate through your appearance, voice and body language must be equal to or better than your resume or application. You must meet and exceed their expectations. The winners do just that.

William Thourlby's observations are even more relevant in today's society. He said: "In a world where 'first impressions' become 'opinionated facts' that control other people's behavior; presence and appearance are skills that are cost effective to every person and company because they not only increase the quality of life in the workplace, contribute to employee morale, and embellish the company image, they play a major role in developing a person's self-image, and in generating profits. The lack of these skills can be highly visible and extremely costly for any person or company in today's marketplace, and they are skills you can't afford to be without."

Susan Bixler, another well respected image authority, said: "If you want the job, you have to look the part. If you want to be promoted, you have to look promotable. If you want respect, you have to dress as well or better than your industry standards."

I can't help thinking for a moment about the movie, The Social Network. In it, Justin Timberlake plays Sean Parker, founder of Napster. He is the well-dressed, well-mannered, suave business networker who helped propel nerdy, ill-mannered, and socially inept Mark Zuckerberg, owner and creator of Facebook played by Jesse Eisenberg, literally from rags to riches! This goes to show that even true genius without "packaging" or the right "image" to present it, won't often succeed to its greatest potential. Genius and creative ideas need packaging and representation just like everything else. That's why most companies have a sales force that often dresses better than the support team. Even to Zuckerberg's meteoric rise, image mattered, even though it definitely wasn't his image. Sean Parker had the image and it got Zuckerberg the financial backing he needed to make Facebook the multi-billion dollar industry it is today.

Getting dressed, without a concrete idea of the effect our image will have, is the same as going to an important meeting without any preparation or idea of what you will be presenting. Being unprepared is not smart and being unprepared with your image is equally "not smart." We really need to wake up! People need to "get" you, read you at a glance and we need to make it easy for them to do that. Never forget that perception is directly connected to reception. There is the power in each of us to manage people's reaction to us.

If communication is image, what is the language it speaks? Here is a chart that I created to help people understand the linguistic cues that the components of their image communicate:

Image = Language
Clothing = Vocabulary
Hair/Makeup = Intonation
Accessories = Punctuation, Exclamation Marks
Body Language = Inflection
Attitude = Volume
Vocal Inflection = Emphasis, Reiteration

The sum of these components forms your "image presence." Now, with this knowledge, I want you to ask yourselves the following questions:

- What image am I projecting?
- Is it helping me reach my goals?
- What image would help my career?
- What image would create better relationships?
- Am I doing the best job I can in packaging myself every day, wherever I go?

Here is a list of the main visual cues (through one's appearance) that we can project to be well received:

- **Detail oriented:** Fitness and grooming is exquisite; added touches of style such as matching socks or hosiery; the right accessories; matching shoes and belt for men; handbag and shoes for women; professionally applied makeup for women; styling products for men's hair; current stylish hair.

- **Trustworthy:** Conservative clothing styles in blues, grays or brown tones, quality fabrics, conservative color combinations, good quality shoes, belts and accessories, understated elegance.

- **Modern:** More trendy fashions, newest hairstyles, avant garde accessories, high fashion shoes, handbags and accessories, edgy and never staid.

- **Successful:** Looking a cut above: Expensive looking designer clothing, well pampered look, fresh glowing complexion, a year round golden tan, white straight teeth, impeccably groomed, relaxed yet energized body language.

"Are you ready to have your image critiqued?" This next exercise will help them in ways they can't yet imagine. Eager, yet afraid, no one volunteers to come up to the front of the class.

"I know that most of you don't know what your image is saying about you. You just know it could be better. So let's come up to the front of the room, one at a time and see what we see! Who wants to be first? Meagan, tell us again what you do for a living. What is your approximate yearly income? How long have you been in this line of work? What is the goal for your image? How did you come dressed here today; for work or for socializing? Is this your normal makeup application and hairstyle? Okay, great. Now turn around slowly and let us see you from all angles."

One by one, I call them up. Within the class we have an array of personalities and professions. We have an artist who looks like a corporate secretary. We have a physician who looks like a sports pro. There is a beauty expert who doesn't look like she feels very beautiful. There is a lawyer who doesn't look successful. There is a fifty-three-year-old woman who looks like she's in her late sixties. There is a professional woman who looks like a party girl. On and on it goes. Few of the women look like what they do for a living. The men's boot camp has the same issues. Very few students ever have it right. They want to say one thing, their images say another.

"Be kind. Remember that we made a promise to uplift one another. But be honest. We can't improve our image if we don't understand how others see us. Tell her. Come on! Does she look like a successful attorney? No? Why not?"

We do this for an hour and all of my students hear my opinion and those of their peers. It is an awakening moment. *"Aren't you all glad that you left your egos in the parking lot?"* I laughingly ask. *"Better to learn this now, then to go on forever misrepresenting yourselves."*

I decide to tell them about an ABC two-part special called *"Lookism"* that was on television many years ago. It was an undercover, hidden camera expose about the prejudices associated with image. ABC sent out two couples for job interviews: One man and one woman were each very well dressed and good looking, with overall great appearances. The other man and woman were not nearly as well dressed, had average appearances and were not as physically good looking. The second pair was actually much more qualified for the job. But it was the better looking, well-dressed man and woman who got hired on the spot, offered higher pay and better benefits packages. When the people who hired them were asked point blank if they hired these people because they looked better, they emphatically said no. They said they **looked** more qualified, had the **look** that they wanted to represent their company, and seemed more confident and able to do the job! Perception is everything, or as one of my clients once told me, "Image, Image, Image. That's all they talked about. My resume never came up!" This same client was offered three and a half times his salary … going from earning $125,000 a year plus benefits to $350,000 a year plus better benefits in only 6 weeks of looking great.

I would say that's a very good reason to take me seriously. Wouldn't you? … As the saying goes, "You never get a second chance to make a first good impression."

CHAPTER SIX

Knowing What Makes You Special

Time to roll up your sleeves and learn the basics of knowing how to package yourselves correctly and effectively. The method I'm about to teach you was designed to help you understand what makes you special: your unique coloring, contrast levels, texture, fashion type, facial shape, and body proportions. This method is simple and it works. If you follow it, step by step, you will become an effective shopper. You'll stop wasting time and money and you'll get great results. Best of all, you will look great and take consistent control over your image. Guesswork gone! Confidence goes up! You get compliments.

"Eve, I hate shopping. I feel so overwhelmed going into stores. I don't know where to begin. I don't know what to try on or how to follow the trends. So I end up either not shopping or buying things in catalogs. It's less painful and I can easily return whatever doesn't look good. Truthfully, I still never look that right and I feel badly about that. I should like to shop, but I hate it," a female student says with her eyes cast downward.

I ask, *"How many of you face the same shopping challenges? How many of you feel that you would get more respect and recognition if only you could package and present yourselves better?"* Most of my students nod yes. It is obvious they are uncomfortable.

"I shop once or twice a year," a boisterous male adds.

"Really, once or twice? That's pretty good for a guy," I say.

"Well, I guess it's more like every 3–5 years, to be honest. I go shopping when my wife complains enough that my clothes look terrible. So I run into a department store, buy what they have on display or what the sales associate likes … buy it in every color and get the heck out of there."

THE GOAL: MIMIC AND FLATTER

The goal of dressing well is to mimic and flatter who you are. We all have a certain coloring, body lines and facial shape. To look our best, we need to know what those key elements are and then mimic them in the colors and clothing shapes we wear. In other words, you enhance your appearance by flattering it with colors, textures, patterns, fabrics, combinations, and silhouettes that resonate to who you really are. Then you find out your fashion type, learn how to follow trends, and shop effectively to create your core wardrobe.

COLOR HARMONY

The first step is to understand your unique color harmony. Your color harmony is the combination of your skin, hair, and eye colors which correspond to the seasons of the year.

In the book, *Eat Right For Your Blood Type*, author Peter J. D'Adamo, shows how people feel better eating certain foods. He has proven that some foods are beneficial (regenerate your body), some are neutral (are just food), and some foods are actually detrimental (cause you harm). Think of colors in the same way. Some colors will make you feel and look great, some will have no special effect and some will make you look sick!!

Without delving into quantum physics, all you need to be aware of is that colors have a direct effect on our emotions. There is a reason that blue is calming while red is exciting. Their frequencies are not the same and they evoke very different emotional responses. A person's coloring also has a unique frequency or vibration which needs to match the colors he or she wears. Why? Because, although many people are not consciously aware of this, the right colors make us feel better. That's why one needs to know what colors resonate to each person.

Color is a vibration. It creates a mood, elicits strong emotions and can draw or repel people to us. Each person, based on his natural color harmony resonates and vibrates to certain colors. Therefore, the colors we wear need to match our own color harmony or we create dissonance and that is not in our best interest. I am certain that all of you have seen someone wear a color that made him/her look sick or jaundiced, and if you think about it, it also made you feel queasy to look at him/her wearing it! In the business world, that could be disastrous … turning off a potential client, boss or buyer! Yet every day many people unknowingly turn people off, simply by the colors they wear.

Your Color Harmony is based on three elements: your natural hair color, your skin tone, and your eye color. Sit down in front of a large mirror, preferably in natural light and really look at your face. First notice your hair color. If you dye it, then think about what color it was when you were ten years old. Next, look at your eyes and find the most descriptive name for their color. For example, don't just call your eyes brown. You need to know what kind of brown. Are they caramel brown, golden brown, dark brown-black, or light olive brown? Really take notice.

Look at your complexion. Is it olive, light or dark, pale ivory, neutral taupe, rosy pink, peachy, caramel, brown, or dark brown (or any variation). Be as descriptive as you can. If you have trouble with this part, ask a close friend or family member to help you describe your coloring. A professional makeup artist at a department store can help you describe your skin and eye color too.

Every person can wear every color. Every color, yes, but not every shade!! This is crucial for you to understand. For example, you can all wear red. But what shade of red? Blue-red, orange-red, brick-red, or coral-red? You can all wear white. But which white? All whites are not the same. Stark white, off-white, beige-white, or yellow-white? No one looks good in every shade. Not even super models or celebrities! Neither do you! Most people don't buy their clothing based on their best colors. They buy them based on the latest trend, which celebrity wore it, if their favorite super model is wearing it, what is on the store mannequin display, and even if their best friend bought it. None of which are good reasons to spend money on colors that don't look good on you! You must know your most flattering color choices or more precisely, your most flattering shades of color.

So many people toss off lines like "I look good in any color" or "I can wear any color I want if I change my makeup." That's simply not true. While it would be great to believe such myths, to find your most flattering colors takes more effort and understanding than buying something because its "in" or your favorite celeb is wearing it.

Let me give you a great example. This year red lipstick is the newest fashion trend. So at this year's Golden Globe awards many actresses were wearing bright red lipstick. But most of them looked terrible in it because they were wearing the wrong shade! I was cringing because they could have looked spectacular if their makeup artist had been more aware of each celebrity's color harmony and put the correct shade on her lips. But that takes more work which is something many people seem unwilling to do.

I can't help but think back to twenty years ago, when my surrogate mom and dear friend (who happens to have been a family counselor and psychologist) Sally, told me, "You know, Evie, what is hard is easy and what is easy is often hard."

To which I said, "What? What on earth do you mean by that?"

Sally said, "Evie, most people want to take the easy way out in life, which usually ends up being more difficult in the long run. But when we take the more difficult path, do things the right way, and really think about what we are doing, we make better choices and that turns out to make our lives easier later on."

Ah, my dear Sally. Truer words were never spoken. In regard to dressing well, the easy way out usually never gives us the best result.

"Eve, why should we care about buying certain colors and not others? Does it really make such a big difference? I don't know anyone who knows their best colors and they look okay. So what's the big deal?" asks Gail. The other women in the room nod in agreement.

Another student raises her hand and asks, "Eve, you don't really want us to walk around stores with those color swatches, do you? I mean no disrespect, but it seems so silly."

"*Good comments! How many of you are wondering the same thing?*" Almost everyone in the room raises her hand. I must tell you that men react to this topic in the same way. They are intrigued with learning about which colors they look good in, but they doubt how important it really is.

Color guidelines are meant to be a general guide. No palette, consultation or guide is meant to replace your own good judgment. You can't just look the part; you have to feel it, too. That means being comfortable in your own skin, as well as what you drape over it. The best thing about doing a color analysis on yourself is that it ties in all functions of your wardrobe: clothing, makeup, and accessories. When all three facets of what you wear are in your color harmony, your wardrobe will fit together like an easy crossword puzzle. It will be truly liberating for you to open your closet because everything will be so easy to mix and match. When you travel, you won't need to take as much, because fewer pieces will create more options.

It's important to remember that colors change each year for spring and fall as new shades and fabrics are invented. If you want to look your best, then you must see how this new shade flatters you and only buy it if it does. In other words, you must know your fashion temperature; whether it's cool or warm and let that guide you.

YOUR FASHION TEMPERATURE

The first step in knowing your color harmony is finding out whether you have cool or warm coloring. Twenty years ago, I attended an image consulting meeting where Louise Elerding of Los Angeles was teaching us about color concepts. Louise's method of explaining about color resonated with me and I have based my teachings on her lecture, along with Carole Jackson, author of *Color Me Beautiful*, Suzanne Caygill, author of *Color The Essence of You* and *Beauty for All Seasons* image and color training.

"I want you to think of the world of color as a sphere." I drew a circle on the flip chart for everyone to see. Then I drew a vertical line down the center of the sphere, dividing it in two halves. *"On the right half we have cool colors. On the left, warm colors. Every person has either cool or warm coloring. Knowing this is crucial.*

"People with cool coloring look best in colors that have blue-red undertones. People with warm coloring look best in colors that have orange-yellow undertones," I say as I look around the room to be certain they are following me. *"Some examples of colors with blue-red undertones are burgundy, sapphire blue, fuchsia, and emerald green. Some warm colors are mustard gold, rust, milk chocolate brown, and olive."*

Next, I draw a horizontal line across the color sphere. *"We now divide the cool side and the warm side into two sections. This gives us a total of four sections to our sphere."*

These sections correlate to the four seasons of the year: Winter, Summer, Autumn, and Spring. The two left quadrants are cool seasons: Winter and Summer. The two right ones are warm: Autumn and Spring. This may seem confusing at first because summer is thought of as a warm time of the year. In color analysis, Summer refers to the colors seen at that season of the year. In that vein, when we think of summer we think of turquoise blue oceans, sandy beaches, clear blue skies and everything washed in bright sunlight. When we think of Winter, we think of an absence of color that comes to life in jewel toned holiday decorations. For Autumn, we think of autumn leaves and for Spring we think of flowers blooming: light and bright.

Therefore, the four sections correspond to the four seasons of the year as follows: Winters and Summers are categorized as cool seasons because they wear "cool" colors which mimic and flatter their cool coloring. Autumns and Springs wear "warm" colors to mimic and flatter their warm coloring. In the simplest terms, think of your fashion temperature as cool or warm. I will get more specific in a moment.

The absolute easiest way to know which seasonal type you are (and your best colors) is the following method. Imagine that you just inherited a beautiful mansion; you have an unlimited budget, and your own interior decorator. Money is no object. You get to start from scratch; everything in the house will be new. What color scheme will you tell the decorator to use? Describe the colors in exact shades. For example, don't just say blue, white and brown. That's too generic. Instead think of the most descriptive exacting shades such as denim blue, off-white and dusty brown. Limit your choice to three colors.

Now before you write this down, really FEEL what it would be like to be surrounded in those colors. Notice if your vibration (your energy gauge) goes up or down. Do these colors make you feel comfortable and energized? If not, dig deeper and really get in touch with your feelings. Many people are so used to compromising that they have forgotten what colors really excite them until they are forced to think about it. All you have to do is align your energy with the powerful energy of your best colors by feeling into it. How color makes you feel is your best gauge and use of your own "inner guidance system" (as coined by Esther and Jerry Hicks in the book, *The Law of Attraction*). If you have been very out of touch with your coloring, then you must let your feelings guide you when you imagine yourself surrounded in certain colors. Why? Because as I said before, color has a vibration that must match with your vibration. When thinking about certain colors ask yourself, "Do you feel better or worse? Happy or sad? Excited or bored? Which shades of color make your heart sing? Therefore, which do you want to be surrounded in every day?"

Every client I have ever posed this scenario to almost always replies with the colors in which they look best. That's because we love to surround ourselves in our favorite colors, which are colors that naturally harmonize with our own color harmony. You see, we all instinctively know our colors. We have just gotten out of touch with them. We never learned to trust ourselves. Now, narrow your focus, hone in on what colors express your inner beauty and match your Fashion Temperature. Watch a power unleash that you never knew you possessed!

Knowing your color harmony will save you from making awkward decisions – and grant you a lifetime pass out of the fashion police jail. If you have cool coloring and you wear warm colors, you will look muddied up or grayed. The reverse holds true for people with warm coloring. To prove this point, I want you all to think back to when you were in elementary school and your teacher gave you a tin of water color paints. We all had that experience of mixing the colors until the result was "mud." At which point we wondered what went wrong. Well, the very same thing happens when a person has cool coloring and they wear all warm colors. They look "muddy." Their complexion dulls down and greys. Their look tired and lackluster. The reverse also happens when people with warm coloring wear cool colors. They diminish their vibrancy. So you see it's really a better idea to know your fashion temperature and follow it.

THE FOUR COLOR SEASONS

Your color season will guide you to the right clothing colors, your most flattering makeup colors, your best hair color choices, and your coordinating accessory colors. You will even want to surround yourselves with the right colors in your home. Why? Because we all feel better when we are surrounded by colors that mimic our own coloring … it feels good. Harmonizing with color is more than just pleasing to the eye. At its core, it's soothing to the soul. It changes the energy you emit to a more positive powerful frequency and it's tangible to you and everyone else.

Another benefit of wearing colors that harmonize with your skin tone and personality is that when people look at you their eyes will go from your face, down and then back up. They will be drawn to you and want to pay attention to what you are saying. If you are wearing colors that aren't right for you, your face will seem disconnected from the rest of you; creating a sort of negative horizontal line under your face that creates a disconnect between your face and body, making it difficult for others to concentrate on what you're saying. You dull down as your natural coloring clashes with the colors you are wearing, creating a dissonance that is difficult to explain, yet tangible to feel.

WINTER SEASONAL TYPE

Most people in this world are Winters, and they have "cool" coloring. Maybe because dark brown hair, brown eyes and neutral skin tone is the most common color combination. Of course, Winters can have other skin, hair, and eye colors, but they are in the minority. Winters are the predominant seasonal type and as such have the easiest time finding their colors in the stores as retailers logically tailor their inventories for the masses.

Let's think about the way the world looks during Winter. Winter is a time for dark starry skies, snow-capped mountains and very little color as most trees and flowers are dormant. The sky is usually grey, dark and cloudy. Things look dreary and lack color. Then after Thanksgiving, the Christmas decorations go up and suddenly the world is full of color and light, which beautifies and brightens everything! Similarly, a person with Winter coloring has very neutral coloring that needs clear pure color to look his/her best. The winter holidays wouldn't look beautiful without the bright colors illuminating them. Like the world in a traditional winter climate, a person with Winter coloring needs color and brightness to come alive!

Let's think of that time of year. How the bright decorations of silver and gold, red, green and blue make all the difference. People with winter coloring look good in the following primary colors of the rainbow: yellow, orange, red, blue, green and violet. These are pure, bright, clear, clean primary colors. They also look great in all of the regal jewel tones: sapphire blue, royal purple, ruby red, and emerald green. They wear all of the classic basic neutral colors: dark black, bright white, charcoal grey, dark navy blue, and true red. Winters can wear brown IF it is a red brown or plum brown like bittersweet chocolate. Their pastel choices are icy and clear. To understand Winter pastel colors, simply imagine taking pint size cans of pure white paint and adding a drop of primary color into each one. Pure red lightens to icy pink, dark navy to icy blue, emerald green to mint green, bright school bus yellow to pale yellow, dark charcoal to diamond grey, etc. Think of the hues in classic button-down men's dress shirt colors.

SUMMER SEASONAL TYPE

The other cool season is Summer. Now think of the way the world looks during summertime. Clear blue skies, sandy beaches, bright sunny days, lots of flowers and lush green, everything bathed in sunlight. Similarly, Summers look wonderful in cool Winter colors that have been bathed/washed with sunlight, so they become softer and less strong. Summers wear the colors of a beautiful tropical beach: soft white, sandy beige, aquatic blues, muted turquoise, sun yellows, taupe, mint greens, lavenders, plums, and rose to name a few. Summers wear all of the winter colors, but in a more muted tone. The intense sunlight bleaches and fades the intensity of the pure Winter colors. Think of emerald green being softened into turquoise green, primary yellow becomes a delicious soft pale yellow, black becomes soft grey, navy becomes denim blue, dark brown becomes taupe, red softens into berry, royal purple becomes plum, bright pink becomes rose, hot pink becomes mauve and icy blue becomes periwinkle. To know which pastels Summers wear, imagine cans of soft-white paint. Simply add a drop of clear bright Winter colors to each can. Pure Winter white becomes dirty white or sun white. Charcoal grey becomes very light blue-grey. Dark navy blue becomes soft aquamarine blue. Hot pink becomes rose pink and khaki becomes oyster beige.

Summers have soft, shimmery coloring. Winter colors would overpower them because they are too strong, clear and bright. Summers need muted cool colors to look their best. Summers remind me of ice cream cones and yummy sherbets. Whether they are brunette, blond or redhead, their coloring is luscious. Summers often think they are Autumns, because both seasons look best in muted colors. Summers wears *muted* cool blue-red based colors, while Autumns wear *muted* warm red-orange based colors.

Summer colors are more difficult to find in the stores, so shopping takes more effort. But the results are worth the extra time!

AUTUMN SEASONAL TYPE

Look now at the other side of our color sphere! The warm rich colors of Autumn. Autumns look like the world during fall. Think of autumn leaves with their variegated browns, red-oranges and gold tones. All autumn colors are warmed and toasted. Autumn-colored people look fantastic in colors that make Winters and Summers look ill. Think I am wrong? Just try to drape a winter or a Summer in mustard, lime green, rust orange, chocolate browns, and camel, to name just a few. You will be shocked at how bad they look. But those same warm colors will make Autumns look vibrant and healthy!! Autumns wear Tuscan warm muted colors. Autumn colors are the Winter pure primary clear colors that have been bronzed, warmed, and toasted. By the way, I am an Autumn and I love those colors so much that I once brought an Autumn leaf to my hairdresser and asked him to make my hair that color!!

For Autumns, pure white becomes cream or beige, dark bittersweet brown becomes milk chocolate brown, bright orange becomes pumpkin, emerald green becomes olive, blue grey becomes yellow grey, pink becomes coral, burgundy becomes brick, and dark shiny black becomes soft black. Autumn pastels are primary colors that have been dropped into cans of beige paint: white mutes and lightens into parchment, primary yellow becomes mustard gold into pale yellow gold, bright orange becomes light peach, emerald green becomes pale khaki, and dark navy becomes pale grey blue.

SPRING SEASONAL TYPE

Springs, the last color season, are the light and bright counterparts of Autumn. Whereas the world in autumn is bronzing, the world in spring is blooming. Everything is awakening. Think of: daffodils, fresh blades of grass, light bright blue skies, violets and lavender, corals and the warm brown earth around flower beds. Springs look terrific in light and bright warm colors … not muted deep warm tones like Autumns. Olive green turns into leaf green, mustard turns into daffodil yellow, pumpkin orange turns into tangerine, reds go brighter, olive drab khaki turns into olive tan, etc. Springs looks like fields of blossoming flowers, their coloring is softly sun-kissed and honeyed. Think of colors at the park.

Springs' pastels are made from those same natural hues. To understand their best pastels, take autumn colors and put a drop in a can of cream colored paint resulting in: yellow grey lightens and brightens into pale yellow grey, mustard gold into buttery soft golden yellow, rust into sherbet orange, and olive into very pale pistachio green. Springs are the rarest season and their colors are the most challenging to find in stores. Coincidentally, one's colors are usually easiest to find during one's season: Spring colors are easier to find from the end of March to June.

FLOW COLORS

"Eve, I know I am a Winter, but I look great in olive green, which is an Autumn color. Can you explain that to me?" one of the women says. "Yeah, I love wearing dark greys and black, but I am a summer. I don't get it," says another.

"Thank you for bringing that up. I am certain many of you like some of the colors from other seasons."

Many years ago, over twenty to be exact, when color theory really became popular, pioneering image consultants began to test color theory more deeply. One of them, named Doris Poosier, who wrote *Always in Style*, came up with the theory of "flow-colors." Flow-colors are colors that you flow from your season into another.

Personally, I was relieved to learn about that, because it made more sense to me than the strict four season guidelines. It made sense that most people have unique coloring that isn't totally confined to one season. Because as human beings, many of us don't fit into a rigid box. We have nuances to our coloring. However, every now and again, I do meet people whose coloring is textbook, smack dab, right into their season ... like a bull's eye. They truly look best wearing their seasonal colors only, because their color harmony is so strong into their season that nothing else would come close to looking as flattering!

If you think of our color sphere with cool Winters and Summers on the left and warm Autumn and Springs on the right, some people fall on the border of another section of the sphere. For example, I am a dark haired Autumn who is on the cusp of Winter. So I look good in a few Winter colors such as royal blue, black and turquoise. Winters that have olive green eyes look great in Autumn olives and khakis. Summers with dark hair also look great in burgundy and dark grey. It's important though, to know your main color season, and that's where your wardrobe should be focused.

Remember, that the entire point of all this is to "flatter and mimic" who you are. Much like a great sound system at a concert amplifies the singer's voice and makes it sound even better, flattering and mimicking who you are in your clothing, accessories, hair and makeup ... makes you look even better. Knowing your seasonal and flow colors is only the beginning. There are other important elements to consider.

CONTRAST

The next vital ingredient of understanding your color harmony is to know your natural contrast levels. This will teach you how much or how little contrast you need to create in your clothing, accessories, hair color and makeup. Every person looks better when he or she mimics their natural levels of contrast. This is something we are born with and will look best if we don't try to change it. Even though you may grey or color your hair, wear makeup and get a tan, your natural contrast levels will always work best on you and should be your lifelong guide.

I learned this theory over twenty years ago in the original *Beauty for All Seasons* method and I have found it invaluable.

There are four distinct levels of contrast:

- Light
- True
- Contrasting
- Vivid

To understand this concept, your contrast levels are determined by the same three elements as your color harmony: your natural skin, hair and eye colors. This time it is a matter of light to dark or "value" levels in your natural coloring. For example, if you have light skin, dark eyes and dark hair, then you have contrasting coloring. However, if you have light skin, light eyes, and light hair then you have light coloring. Let's understand the four categories in more depth.

Light coloring: light hair, light eyes and light skin tone. These people look best dressed in light, soft colors. Their makeup should also be lightly applied in soft colors. Think of porcelain, silky, peaches and cream complexions, light blue or green eyes with pale blonde or silver hair. Light coloring is the rarest of all the four categories. Think of celebrities like Charlize Theron and Heather Graham.

True coloring: medium hair color, medium eyes and medium skin tone. These people look best when dressed in monochromatic colors with very little contrast. Tonal is the key word for people with this contrast level. "Trues" (as they are referred to) are the ones who look best wearing matching tops and bottoms or a suit with a shirt and tie in a very similar shade. Their makeup should be in the most natural, neutral tones. Too much makeup will make them seem ghoulish. Think of golden skin with sun-kissed hair coloring or warm brown skin with medium brown hair. Think of Jessica Biel and Vanessa Williams.

Contrasting coloring: light skin, dark hair, and dark eyes or light hair, light skin, with dark/deep eyes. This person can also have light eyes with dark hair, and lighter skin. Eyes can be dark brown, hazel, green or blue; but they must be deep or bright, creating intensity. This kind of person has at least one contrasting element between his/hers skin, hair, and eye tone. People with contrasting coloring come to life when they wear colors that contrast with one another. Unlike people with true coloring, matching colors from head to toe is not their friend. They look fabulous in dark suits with light shirts or blouses such as black and white or brown with cream. Wearing light or bright colors with dark colors, (even strong bright prints) mimics their strong levels of contrast. Their makeup must also create contrast in at least one area: either strong eye makeup or strong lipstick. Most people on this planet have contrasting coloring. Think of Demi Moore or Elizabeth Taylor.

Vivid coloring: dark hair, dark eyes and dark skin tone. These people look best in strong, bright and vivid colors. They can wear the boldest color of all seasons and never look overwhelmed by it. Their makeup needs to be strong and bold, otherwise they will seem like they aren't even wearing makeup. Think of beautiful brown and black coloring; darker Hispanic, Indian, African American, Middle Eastern coloring. Think of Oprah and Michelle Obama.

It is extremely powerful to know your seasonal color type and your contrast level. You will not only know what colors you look best in, but how much or how little contrast you need to create in your hair, makeup, accessories and clothing choices. All of which makes you look more powerful, polished and pulled together. Plus it takes more of the guesswork out of looking great!

It is important to note that if you color your hair, you will always look best choosing colors that will keep you in your natural contrast level and season. For example, if you are a Winter with natural brown-black hair, you can opt to become a blonde if you go platinum blonde or choose chunky blonde highlights. You still need your hair color to be dramatic. Again, always remember "high to low" contrast and your color will not fight against your natural levels. Makeup is approached in the same way. No matter what the trend, a contrasting woman needs at least one element of her makeup to be bold and strong: her lipstick color, eyeshadow or eyeliner. Bold brows work well for this type of contrasting woman.

I remember when I first learned these theories while I was in training to become an image consultant. I decided to test the color and contrast level theory. I bought a gorgeous new warm chocolate brown pantsuit, with two blouses; one in a matching brown and one in cream. The next day I wore all brown to work; matching suit and blouse. Although the color and fit was perfect, I didn't get one compliment all day! The next week, I wore the same brown suit, this time with the contrasting cream silk blouse. Well, I couldn't believe the amount of compliments I got! The only difference was the contrast that the cream blouse created which mimicked and flattered my own contrast levels; super powerful and so overlooked!

TEXTURE LEVELS

Now that you know your color harmony and contrast levels, the next part of this puzzle is knowing your texture levels. Texture has a strong resonance that must match with what we put on our bodies, in order for us to *feel* good in our clothing choices. This is the tactile part of the equation. I want you to think of your "natural" hair and complexion. Is your hair naturally smooth and silky? Or is it curly and frizzy? Or somewhere in between? What about your complexion and skin tone? Is it smooth and clear or is it freckled and uneven? Remember, all of this is not a judgment call. There is no good or bad. It just is … in other words, you are what you are. All I ask is that you get in tune with it and mimic it in your clothing and accessories.

If your hair and skin are smooth then you need to wear fabrics that are also smooth: supple silks, satins, jerseys, super fine woolens, soft supple cottons, smooth cashmeres, calfskin leathers, etc. However, if your hair is curly and your skin is freckled or uneven in tone, then you will feel best in textured fabrics: crisp sharp pleats, tweed or herringbone woolens, cotton broadcloth, embroidered and embellished textiles, heavier linens, etc. Some people have a texture that has both elements: smooth and textured. They will do best to wear both smooth and textured mimicking their own subtle mix and nuances.

The goal of all of this knowledge is to bring your unique attributes to life. You finally get to be in control of your image, no more colors that wash you out, no more guessing if your makeup choices flatter you, no more hair colors that dull you down or overpower you, and no more fabrics that make your skin crawl! If you think for a moment that this won't make a difference in your life, then think again.

JEWELRY

Jewelry has a color resonance just like clothing. Gemstones and metal colors have seasonal color choices and their contrast levels must be consistent with yours. Metal colors are either cool or warm. The cool metals are white gold, platinum, silver, pewter, and black gold. The warm metals are: pale yellow gold (14K American), bright yellow gold (18K usually Italian and South American), intense orange gold (22–24K Turkish, Middle Eastern or Asian), bronze, and copper. The key to selecting the right jewelry is to choose both the metal and the stones that resonate to your color harmony, levels of contrast, texture, facial shape, outer line and personality. Combine that with your bone structure and fashion type and you can easily hone in on very flattering jewelry. The key here as with all of my teachings about image, is to "know yourself."

As far as gemstones, pearls and semi-precious stones, the rules of color harmony apply. Winters look dazzling in white diamonds, white pearls, black pearls, rubies, blue sapphires, emeralds, onyx, hematite, and lapis lazuli to name a few. Summers look gorgeous in shimmering pink diamonds, creamy off-white or pink pearls, aquamarine, lilac jade, iolite, chalcedony ivory, opals, and other soft cool colored stones. Autumns look stunning in cream pearls, blue-grey Tahitian pearls, canary yellow diamonds, agate, topaz, purple tanzanite, deep amethyst, peridot, citrine, tigers eye, carnelian, muted green turquoise, and other warm rich stones. Springs look lovely in soft yellow pearls, coral, beryl, chrysoprase, yellow quartz, tsavorite garnet, and other light lively bright stones.

Most Winters look best in cool metals with white gold, platinum and silver being the most flattering. However, some Winters who have olive skin tones, hazel or green eyes look great in pale yellow gold too. Again the idea is to mimic your color harmony in everything you wear, including your jewelry.

Those of you who have pure winter coloring would be best to avoid that deep yellow colored gold. It is too orange for your coloring. It is possible to have your yellow gold pieces replated at a fine jewelry store. They can coat it in rhodium and it turns into white gold. Of course, another option is to mix your metals and wear some white gold jewelry alongside your yellow gold pieces to tone them down. Europeans do this all the time.

Summers actually look great in two-toned gold: some white gold and some soft pale yellow gold. This is the only season that really does. The occasional "very golden" Summers look beautiful in all yellow gold, but that is more rare.

Autumns wear warm metals. Autumns look fabulous in 18K Italian gold, intense 20–24K gold, bronze, and copper. Autumns that flow into winter can also wear burnished silver or pewter especially mixed with gold such as David Yurman, Judith Ripka or James Hardy jewelry.

Springs also wear warm metals, but lighter and brighter than their Autumn counterparts, when they can find them. Autumns look better in intense warm metals and springs wear the lighter warm toned metals. It's just a matter of training your eyes to see and feel the difference.

Your seasonal coloring will determine much of jewelry choices. Always remember, "MIMIC AND FLATTER." The jewelry you choose to wear should mimic your color harmony and facial shape, repeat your texture levels, and flatter your contrast levels.

You must be tired of endless shopping trips, filling bag after bag with the latest, greatest fashions only to wind up with a great, big pile of "what was I thinking" once you got home? You must feel bad to have lots of clothing in your closet and still feel like you have nothing to wear! Wouldn't it be nice to walk into a store with confidence and properly select only those items that brought out the best in you? What you have just learned, your colors and the first elements of "what makes you special," will save you tens of thousands of dollars over a lifetime, hours of frustration and literally take the guess work out of dressing yourself. You will be able to buy less and have more. You will be able to afford quality and finer clothing because you will know how to invest in your wardrobe the right way; the way that will bring you a great return on your investment by enhancing your beauty, raising your self-esteem, and increasing your personal power and presence. Let's move forward now and learn the remaining piece of the puzzle, your unique shapes.

CHAPTER SEVEN

Your Unique Facial Shape and Body Proportions

Looking your best is knowing your unique facial shape and body proportions. This knowledge will take the mystery out of dressing well and streamline your shopping time. Your unique facial shape and skeletal structure forms the science of your accessory and apparel choices. The artistic part of the equation flows more easily after the scientific formulas are followed: through your color, style, and fashion choices.

If you think of your color harmony, contrast levels, and texture as the artistic palette that paints your personal style, then your facial shape and proportions are the canvas and frame that you will paint on. One is color, one is shape. We need both elements to be correct in order to look our best.

As all things in the realm of appearance, you need to really look at yourself with objective eyes. We've all heard the phrase "people often listen, but they don't really hear." The same holds true for our person. We look at ourselves in the mirror every day of our lives, but we don't really see what is in front of us.

YOUR FACIAL SHAPE

Every single person, male or female, has either an *angled* or *contoured* facial shape. Of course, our faces do not always fall only into one category, as some people's faces have elements of both shapes. However, it is the dominant facial shape that teaches us what we need to know for dressing and looking our best. Our goal is to mimic our primary facial shape and add elements of the secondary to everything we wear. Most people have no idea what their facial shape is. Years ago, I didn't either.

"Personal power through personal style creates global impact! Did you hear me? The implications of this are huge! You are learning not just how to dress yourselves!!"

I almost shout. *"You are learning to wake up and take your personal power back through the TOTAL knowledge of what makes you unique and special! How many of you know your facial shape?"* In a room of eighteen women, only two people raise their hands. *"Well then, how many of you have ever looked in the mirror?"* Everyone laughs. *"How the heck can you dress yourselves well if you don't even know what you are all about? I mean, really!"*

There are five angular facial shapes and five contoured.

ANGLED FACIAL SHAPES:

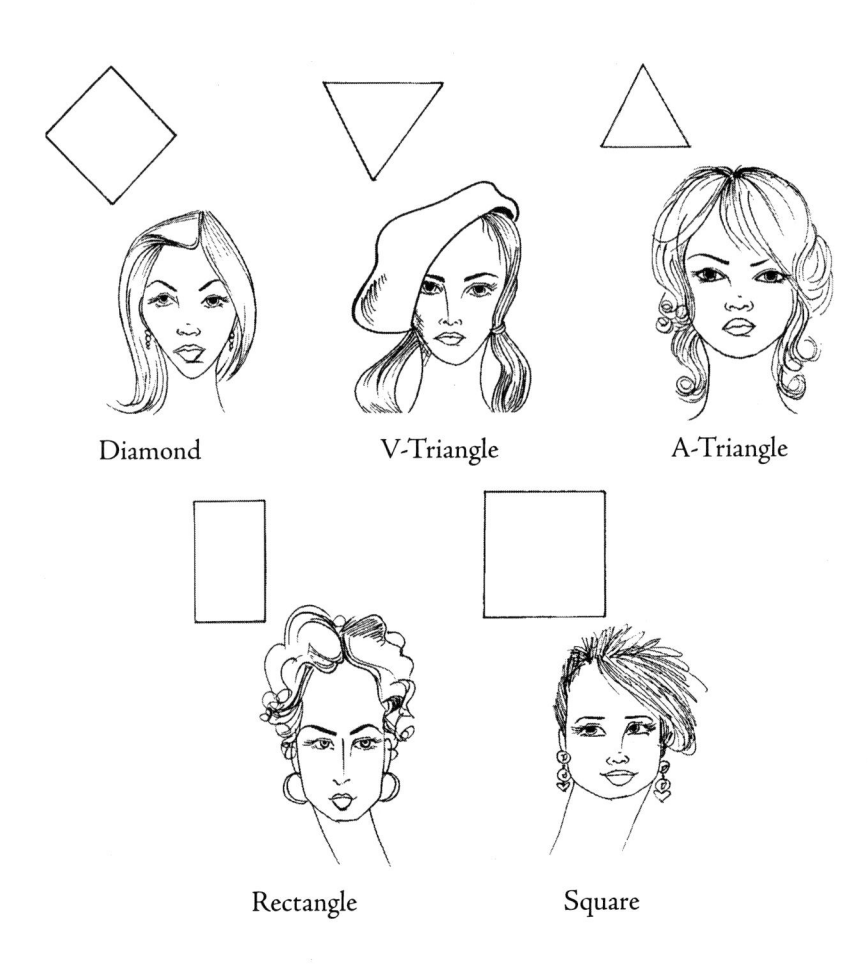

Diamond   V-Triangle   A-Triangle

Rectangle   Square

CONTOURED FACIAL SHAPES:

Heart   Oblong   Pear

Oval   Round

    The easiest way to determine your facial shape is to first pull your hair off your face and forehead completely. Straight back. You can use a hair band if you'd like to. Your forehead shape is a big factor in your facial shape and it can't be ignored by keeping it covered. Next, take a ruler and hold it up to the sides of your face. Are the lines of your face straight and angular like the ruler or do they curve and contour? Then refer to the facial shape chart. If you have an angled face, then look at the five angular shapes. If you have a curved face, then look at the five contoured facial shapes. Find which facial shape has the most similarities to your facial shape by focusing on the widest and narrowest parts of your face that are most similar to the drawings and select one. If you have trouble deciding, look at all ten shapes and have at least one other person help you. A big clue as to whether you are angled or contoured is to think about whether you look best in v-neck or round necklines, stripes or soft florals, pointy toed shoes or round.

"Eve, we can't figure out my facial shape. Everyone says I am angular. But I don't seem to fit any of the five shapes exactly," Lucy says.

"Okay, let's take a closer look. Some people are a combination of two shapes and that's okay. The most important thing to know is your primary shape, if you are angled or contoured, and then your secondary shape. For example: I have an angular facial shape. I am a rectangle. However, I do have some softness to my face. Therefore I will look best in angular lines, with some softness. Can you all see that?" I say as I pull my hair straight back, away from my face.

"So what does this mean? What does our facial shape tell us?"

Everyone is fascinated and eager to know what shape their faces are.

"For those of you who are confused or can't figure out your facial shape, another way to confirm your facial shape is to look at the shape of your fingertips and fingernails. Are you fingertips more round or square? If you are in tune with your lines, then your nails will mimic your facial shape being angled or contoured. Just like your 'imaginary mansion' helped you get in touch with your coloring. Your preferred fingernail shape will help you understand your facial shape. This is accurate most of the time.

"For example, until I had this training, throughout my entire life people told me I had an oval face. But I hated oval nails and scoop necklines and curved patterns. I liked angles! When I finally learned that I actually have a rectangular facial shape it was liberating! It was truly one of those 'ah ha' moments! It made sense of why I love angled handbags and squared off nails and prefer v-necks to round necklines. Everything I had naturally intuited about my style choices started to have a rhyme and a reason."

I believe that every person innately gravitates towards the shapes that mimic his or her facial shape and body proportions. We intuit our best choices when left to our own devices. However, we don't live in a bubble and most of us have learned not to trust our intuition. We give up our power thinking that everyone else knows better what is best for us.

YOUR INNER LINE

Your facial shape determines your *inner line*. Your inner line is either angled or contoured just like your face. Your inner line will tell you many important things. Your inner line determines: your best collar shapes, your most flattering necklines, your best jewelry shapes, your belt buckles, your lapel shapes, your prints and patterns, your shoe shapes, your handbag or briefcase shapes, your best hairstyle options, your eyeglass shapes, your hosiery and sock patterns. The goal is to MIMIC your facial shape through the shape of the inner parts of your clothing and the shoes styles, patterns and accessories you wear. This creates a harmony between what you wear and who you are. Just as wearing colors in your season creates a harmony with your natural coloring ... wearing the right shapes and patterns creates a harmony with your facial shape. Think of your facial shape as the top of the arrow that goes up from your feet through to the top of your head.

With all this in mind, everything you wear on the inside of your body must point back to, and harmonize with, your facial shape. If it does, a powerful synergy is created as your facial shape is repeated throughout what you wear. If not, the power of your presence is diminished as the inner lines of your apparel clash with your natural inner shape. This concept is profound in its simplicity. When you wear the right inner lines, the difference is tangible. Your energy goes up as your appearance is more reflective of who you are.

"I want you all to think about *your facial shape*. Think about the shapes and patterns of the clothing and accessories you love. Are they angled or contoured? Do you resonate to the shapes that match your facial shape? Allow me to demonstrate. Kathy, would you please stand up and come up here so everyone can see you? Okay, Kathy, what is your facial shape? Diamond? Great! Is diamond angled or contoured?" I ask her.

"Angled." Kathy replies.

"*Therefore what is your inner line?*" I ask.

"Angled?" asks Kathy.

"YES! That's right. Your inner line is angled. That means that you look best in angular shapes, patterns, shoes, collars, lapels, jewelry, hairstyles, etc. Can you see that now?" I ask as I look at her. I continue. "Kathy. What kind of handbag are you carrying today?" Kathy holds up an angular structured handbag. "Why isn't it soft and round, like a hobo bag?" I ask her.

"Oh, I hate soft bags. I have always liked structured hard edged handbags, but never knew why," she answers.

"What about Kathy's shoes today? They are pointed-toed pumps. Is that angled or contoured?" I ask the other students.

"Angled!" someone shouts out.

"Precisely. Kathy, do you like round-toed shoes as a rule?" I ask her.

"NO! I hate them. But I never knew why." Kathy says. But then I look at her belt. She is wearing a large belt at her waist with a big round buckle.

"Everyone, take a careful look at how Kathy is dressed today. Is there something that seems out of harmony in her outfit? Somewhere your eyes get 'stuck' as you look at her from head to toe?" I insist.

Lucy runs up and points to Kathy's belt, "The round belt buckle. I got stuck on that. It doesn't look like it belongs on her. It's distracting."

"The big round belt buckle creates a disconnect (or as I like to call it, a disharmony) because it isn't consistent with Kathy's natural born essence and angles. In fact, it is the opposite shape."

You see, the purpose of wearing clothing, shoes, patterns and accessories that mimic your inner line is to create a harmony in your appearance for two main reasons: first, so that you feel fantastic in everything you wear and second, so that people will look at your face, scan downward to your shoes, then quickly look back up to your face to hear your message. They will do that only if your appearance is in harmony with who you are. Like a beautiful concerto, the underlying musical theme is repeated throughout which serves as the thread that holds the music together. The same applies to our image. Our facial shape pattern must be repeated throughout our appearance to hold it together in the same beautiful way.

The principles of the art and science of dressing well, when adhered to, will take the confusion and guesswork out of your wardrobe which will free you up to be more artistic in the expression of who you are (and who you are wanting to become).

THERE'S NO RIGHT OR WRONG INNER LINE

It's interesting to note that years ago (up until the late 90s) we tried to make people adhere to the crazy notion that every person must strive to have an oval facial shape. As if there was something wrong with all other facial shapes, we were taught that we needed to do everything we could through our hairstyle, eyeglasses and makeup to give the illusion of having an oval shaped face. This was impossible to achieve and sent a very negative message, that our natural facial shape, other than the perfect oval, was defective. The newer school of image consulting that I subscribe to says that you mimic and flatter the facial shape you were born with. You don't try to change it, as there are no right or wrong shapes, with the goal being to simply flatter, mimic and repeat whatever your natural facial shape is. So liberating and empowering!

The very same concept applies to our body proportions (figure type). Back in the day, we were taught that every woman had to have an hourglass figure and every man had to have a wedge physique. Science shows us that it is impossible. Our shape is determined by our skeletal (bone) structure. Our muscle mass and fat cells can alter the size and width of certain areas, but not our basic outlying shape. Our job is to know the shape we were born with and dress it the best way we can by flattering our skeletal structure with similar repetitive shapes (Outer Line).

LAPELS, COLLAR SHAPES, NECKLINES, AND PATTERNS

As you are more aware of your inner line, it will be easier to distinguish between angular and contoured lapels, collar shapes, necklines, print patterns, accessories, shoes, handbags, jewelry and more. When selecting a jacket, shirt, blouse, sweater or dress, be careful to choose the necklines and collars that mimic your inner line and flatter your facial shape. Repeating your exact facial shape is the most powerful choice for your necklines or accessories but that isn't always easy to do. The most important thing is to buy items that repeat your inner line. Even tie and print patterns will look better in your correct inner line. Angular collars have points and angles. Contoured collars are rounded. Angular prints are stripes, checks, plaids, and pointed geometric designs and graphic angled florals. Contoured prints are swirls, circles, loops, soft florals and polka dots. Once you train your eye to spot your inner line choices, shopping will be so much easier and effective. The idea is to reduce your stress and look your best.

EYEGLASSES

In this same regard, we select eyeglasses and sunglasses to mimic our own facial shape and inner line. Oval faces wear oval eyeglasses or some combination that includes an oval or contoured line. Squares wear squared and angular eyewear. Rounds wear round and so on. Of course, there are subtle variations to this as I more closely study a client's face. I try to style them in eyeglasses that pick up their predominant facial shape and all its subtleties. For example, a square face that leans toward being a rectangle might get an angular rectangular frame with a squared off line in it. An oval face that has a squared off chin might look best in an oval frame with straight sides. The goal is to mimic, flatter and repeat our own natural shapes, not hide them. It is easy once you learn to pay close attention to your facial shape with all its nuances and match the eyewear to your own shapes. You will be astounded at the huge difference it makes. Your eyeglasses will look great every time. Just take the time to find the right pair.

SHOES, HANDBAGS, AND BRIEFCASES

Your inner line (facial shape) will help you buy your best shoe shape. Contoured facial shapes look best in rounder-toed shoes with softer lines. Angled facial shapes like more pointed toes, squared off toes and more sharply angled shoe shapes. Think of crisp lines versus softer curves. It is not a matter of masculine vs. feminine. Men's shoes can have rounder-toe shapes or more angled ones, all you have to do is notice the vast selection of shoe shapes offered and hone in on the ones that match your inner line. Pay attention to your energy levels when you try on a certain shoe shape. The right shoe will make your energy go up.

Use the same principles when you select a handbag, briefcase, wallet or portfolio case. It works every time. Really look at the buckles and hardware. You'll have choices there too. Belt buckles for men and women come in all shapes: squares, rectangles, round, and oval to name a few of the predominant ones available. Your job is to notice and choose the right shapes for you. Be discerning.

JEWELRY SHAPES

When buying jewelry it's very important to consider your inner line. You will always look and feel better when wearing jewelry that matches and mimics your facial shape. Therefore, always find jewelry in your facial shape, and then find the right color metal and stones. This makes it easier to sift through the huge selection of jewelry most stores offer. Don't forget to consider your contrast and texture levels as well as your fashion type for the very best result.

WOMEN'S OUTER LINE

Now I want us to move on to the discussion of our "Outer Line," which is the other large part of this equation. It is almost the last piece of the puzzle that will help you appreciate what makes you special. Your bodyline refers to your basic skeletal structure. It is NOT about your weight! It is about the relationship between your shoulders, waist and hips. This concept applies to both men and women.

In the Beauty For All Seasons method, (one of the companies I originally trained with), they divided our body type into three main categories. Unlike the well known "body shape" theory, this concept is based entirely on one's skeletal structure, not where you carry your weight. Instead of body type, they refer to it as one's "Outer Line." I have found this to be an easy-to-grasp concept that is consistently accurate. The goal of knowing your Outer Line is to FLATTER your bone structure with your clothing silhouettes. Again, we pair like shapes with like. Let's begin with the female shapes.

The three female Outer Lines are:

CURVED

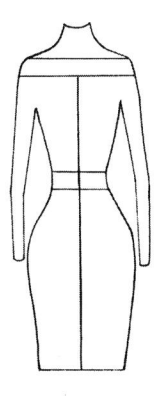

Women with a Curved Outer Line have an hourglass shape. They are curvy. Their bust and their hips are at least 12 inches (or more) fuller than their waistline. A curved body type needs to show definite waistline emphasis to look her best. Curved women need to emphasize the shoulder line and curves of their body by bringing attention to her smaller waist. She needs to dress in clothing that shows off her waist (mimics it) and flatters her curves. Curved women can easily find clothing to suit their curves as long as they remember to show them off. If they don't show their waistline, they will actually look much heavier! They may end up looking frumpy, like a "sack of potatoes" if they wear baggy tops or full loose dresses. Belts and inset waistlines are their best friends.

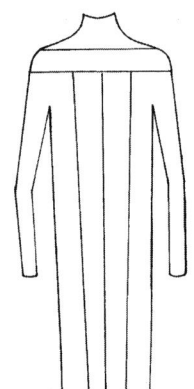

LINEAR

Women with a Linear Outer Line have a straight waistline, no matter how thin they are. Basically, they don't really have a waist and they're wise not to try and create one. Again, this concept is not about weight. It's about skeletal structure. Linear women need to select clothing shapes that emphasize the shoulder line and skims over their waist then narrows near their knees, drawing attention to their lovely slim legs. Some linear women can dress to give the "illusion" of a waistline through dresses that pleat diagonally across their waist, but this is difficult to do properly and requires a high degree of skill. Therefore they are best to draw the eye to their legs and away from their waist. Linear women should mimic their body type by wearing straight cut tops, jackets and dresses that skim their body rather than hug it tightly. Their hemlines can usually go shorter and the bottom of their skirts and dresses look best when penciled in towards the body. Linear women have the most challenging time of dressing right for their body type. Women with this body type need to fight the temptation to wear waistline belts and boxy jackets that end near the waist. They usually look best in jackets that end below the waist, again, drawing the eye to their slimmer hips. Some linear women can wear a belt low slung on their hips, but never on their waist as that will make them look heavier, distorting their proportion and drawing the eyes away from their best features: their shoulder line and legs.

CURVILINEAR

That leads me to the last and most common category, Curvilinear. These women are neither curved nor linear. They are somewhere in between. Curvilinear women can wear some waistline emphasis and look good in it. The caveat is that they look best when they wear their belts and clothing a bit loose and not cinched in or super tight at the waist. This is because their rib cage is not very narrow like a curved hourglass woman. Curvilinear body types need to select clothing that emphasizes their shoulders, waist and hips softly without over emphasis. So if they wear their belts and dresses super tight to the ribcage and waistline, they can risk looking heavier not slimmer. Curvilinear women look great in almost any style that curves softly or glides onto the body. Ultra thin clingy fabrics are not their best choice as those fabrics will tend to grab the waistline. Curvilinear women are the easiest bodyline to dress and find clothing for.

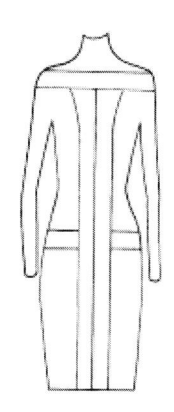

I go on to demonstrate the different body types by asking the women of each category to come to the front of the room. Once again, I find that each woman intuitively knows what she looks best in.

I instruct my students to help one another figure out their bodyline. This helps them see their own shape as well. Curved women usually know that they are curvy. Linear women usually know they don't have a waist. Curvilinear women have the most difficult time understanding their category because there are Curvilinear women who have more defined waists and those who don't. There is a wider variance in this body type: from almost no waistline to being closer to a curved body type. A quick and easy test is to put a 2–3 inch wide belt on a woman. If she looks worse with a tightly cinched in belt, then she is curvilinear, not curved. The easiest determining factor is to look from behind, where you can often see how much or how little waistline emphasis a woman has. Curvilinear body types have a more boyish waistline, even if they are very slender and are super feminine. Again, always remember this is about your body line … which is neither good nor bad. It just is what it is.

Now please look, again, at the Face Shape and Female Body Charts on pages 74–75 and 81–83.

This will help you understand how you put it all together. Note that for each body type you will have either an angled or a contoured facial shape combination. The easiest way to remember how to use this when selecting what to wear is simply: flatter your outside line and mimic your inner line. It is really quite simple once you practice being more aware of your unique shapes. Once again, the goal is to mimic (repeat) your facial shape on your face and down the center of your body, then flatter your outer line by matching the same shape as yours on the outside lines of your clothing.

MEN'S FACIAL SHAPES

In my Men's Overhaul Programs, I teach about Inner Line and Outer Line. Facial shapes are the same for both sexes: angular or contoured.

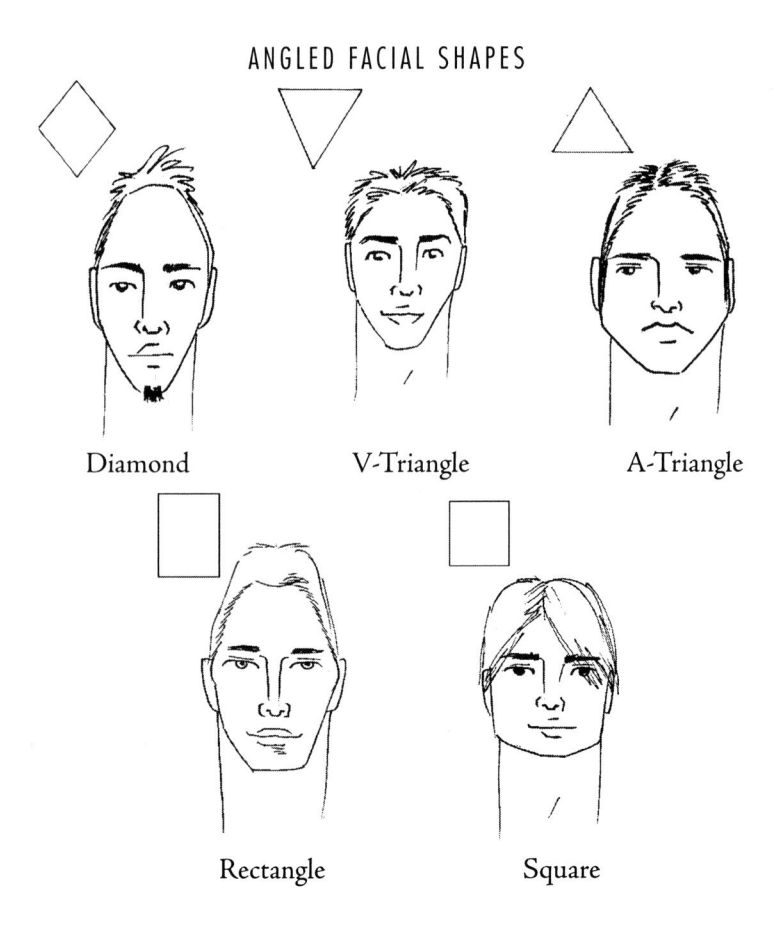

ANGLED FACIAL SHAPES

Diamond   V-Triangle   A-Triangle

Rectangle   Square

DRESS CODE • 85

CONTOURED FACIAL SHAPES:

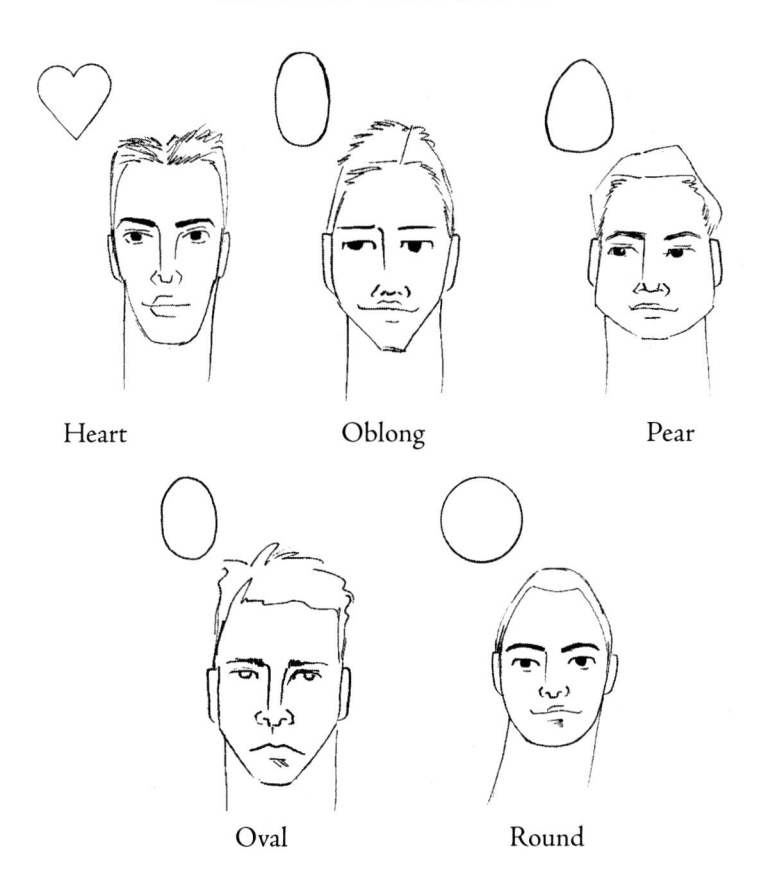

Heart   Oblong   Pear

Oval   Round

MEN'S OUTER LINE

While men also have three Outer Lines, their skeletal structure is very different. The three male categories are the Wedge, the Parallel, and the Relaxed Outer Line.

WEDGE

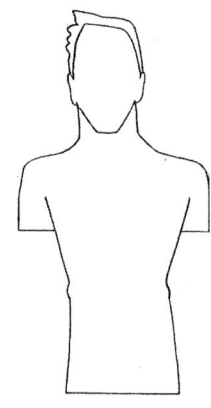

In this category, the upper body volume is larger than the lower body volume. The Wedge man has pronounced shoulders, a slimmer waist and hips. In other words, his outer line looks like a wedge. He can be tall or short, heavier or slim. This is about his proportions from his shoulders to his hips. They create an inverted triangle. This type of man needs to show off his slimmer waist and larger shoulders by wearing clothing that is tapered to mimic and flatter his bodyline. He should opt for clothing that is "fitted," "athletic," or "European" cut. This cut of suit enhances his Wedge body shape with its tapered waist. No vents in the back enhance the narrow hips. A low button stance focuses attention to the waist and hips.

PARALLEL

Men who have a Parallel Outer Line have shoulders and hips that are fairly balanced/equal. In other words, the upper and lower body volume is approximately the same. Their skeletal structure is straighter up and down. This body type looks best in the Updated British American or Traditional cut of clothing. This cut enhances the Parallel body shape with its moderate tapering at the waist, mid-button stance and balanced design. The predominance of men in this country have traditional outer lines. They look best in clothing that skims their body, but is not too fitted in the middle.

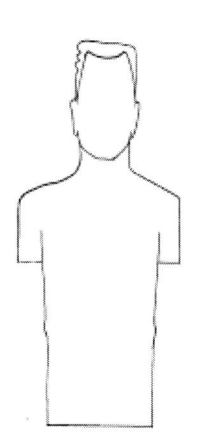

RELAXED

The Relaxed body's lower body volume is larger than his upper body volume. He is the opposite of the Wedge. He usually has athletic thighs and a fuller rear end. His best clothing style is the Ivy League cut which enhances his Relaxed body shape with its strong vertical lines falling from the shoulder. The high buttons also create a slenderizing vertical line. Relaxed body shapes should keep color and pattern emphasis directed at their upper body.

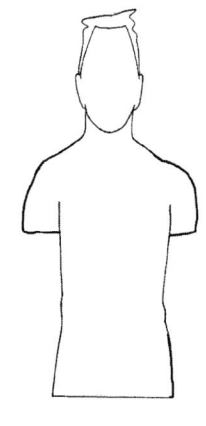

The men are fascinated with all of this information in their overhaul programs. They are amazed that a collar shape can make such a difference to their facial shape or that there is a scientific reason why their bodies look better in certain shapes versus others. They love the formulas they can follow to empower and enhance their image. Bravo to the men of this world who realize that there's more to shopping than saying, "I'll take that dress shirt in a 15½ x 32 in three colors, when it's been twenty years since they fit into a 15½."

ACCENTUATE OR CAMOUFLAGE

I believe that people look better and feel much more comfortable when they consciously make the effort to MIMIC their facial shape, FLATTER their body line and REPEAT their color harmony in what they wear. This is done through our choices. You get to decide in this method what areas of your face and body people focus on when they see you. In other words, we get to "Accentuate" or "Camouflage" any part of our body or face. In other words, we can draw *attention to* or *away from* any area.

Accentuating is really just another way of saying "highlighting" while camouflaging actually means to "hide or diminish." In my opinion it's easier to draw attention; for example, if you want to draw attention to your upper body, but not your lower body, wear a lighter, brighter, patterned jacket with simple dark solid pants. The eye will go to the pattern and color while the dark color will recede almost as if it's not there.

This concept is one that is based on artistic principles. An artist always chooses what subject he or she wants the viewer to notice. Modigliani's famous painting of the woman with the long neck was an obvious choice to accentuate her swan-like neck. Another artist may have chosen to put the same woman in a tall ruffled collared blouse or in a tall choker style necklace to camouflage her tall neck. Either choice can be very beautiful.

I'll never forget one of my boot camp students, named Linda. She was tall and had a very thin upper body with a significantly fuller lower area. The difference from top to bottom was about 2 dress sizes. She was very self-conscious about her fuller hips although she had a beautiful stately body. She tried to camouflage it at all times. While we were shopping for her new wardrobe, I found her a sexy black matte jersey dress that hugged her entire body tightly. The stretchy fabric was gathered across the body. Linda said there was absolutely no way she would look good in that dress with her "full hips!" I insisted she try it on. Two minutes later she emerged from the fitting room walking around the boutique like she was a "diva" goddess that had fallen from the heavens! Linda couldn't believe that she could look so sexy showing off her full hips. What she found out was that she could dress that way for a date with her husband or to a special evening event. She learned that she could choose to accentuate her figure and that was extremely empowering to her self-esteem. We always have a choice when we know how to dress ourselves.

When accentuating, I strongly recommend you only draw attention to 2–3 areas of your outfit or people won't know where to rest their eyes when they look at you. For example, you can draw attention to your bust and arms or legs and waist or neckline and hips. If you have a great figure you can highlight your bust, waist, hips and legs. But very few women can do that right and look classy. It's fun to think of your outfit each day as a piece of art that strives to achieve color harmony, balance, and proportion. Accentuating or camouflaging is a part of that equation. As in art, it is the empty spaces that naturally highlight the rest. With that in mind, camouflaging can be seen as the empty space that draws the eye elsewhere.

For more detailed information on body proportions and figure challenges, there are many books you can study. One of these books, that I like, is called "The Look" by Randolph Duke. It has some very valuable information that is easy to follow and has a unique approach. To me, body proportion is a matter of common sense. I think we all know if we are long-waisted or short-waisted. For example, if you are short-waisted, wear longer tops and jackets to give the illusion of length. If you are long-waisted do the opposite. If you have full hips and don't want to bring attention to their fullest part, I suggest your jacket end above or below your widest area. And avoid wearing ruffles, pleats, and pockets where you want to look slimmer.

We accentuate or camouflage areas of our body through the use of color, fit, patterns, fabrics, textures, seams, pleats, gathers, buttons, pockets, and accessories. Bright or light colors draw attention to an area, because light brings out and dark recedes. Therefore, if you have a large abdominal area, you would opt for darker colors for shirts or tops and lighter brighter colors on the bottom, where you are slimmer. The reverse is true. If you carry more of your weight in your legs and have a slim torso, then draw the eye to your torso and wear solid, simple, medium to dark colors on your legs. Tight fabrics draw focus, while looser fabrics disguise. Anything that adds thickness or girth such as thick fabrics, double sewn seams, contrast top stitching, flap pockets, contrasting buttons, pleats or gathers make areas of your body look fuller or accentuates them. This works well to make bustlines or chests look larger, rear ends bigger, and shoulders stronger.

It's very important to use caution when opting to wear loose clothing. If you wear your clothing too loose, you run the risk of looking larger and heavier. Although you may think the opposite is true. Very flowy loose tops, pants, skirts and dresses often look best on tall thin women (as long as their figure is seen somewhere). There is a big difference between fabrics that drape or skim over the body to fabrics that either balloon out or hang like a tent. People who want to look thinner tend to make themselves look heavier by wearing very loose shapeless clothing. No matter what you weigh (unless you are extremely obese) it is always best to highlight or accentuate at least one of your slimmer areas (even if it's only your wrist and neck) by drawing focus to them. It is also helpful to flatter the size of your bone structure by wearing prints and patterns that are proportional to your size. Larger/taller people can look out-of-balance with little tiny print patterns. The reverse is true for petite women and smaller men. They would look out of proportion wearing huge prints and patterns.

YOUR FASHION TYPE

The last part of this equation is knowing your fashion type. Most people are a mix of two or more fashion types. People sometimes vary their fashion type depending on where they're going. It's crucial to find your "look." Everyone needs a style that represents who they are. Anna Wintour, editor of Vogue and the most powerful woman in fashion opts for an iconic classic bob as her hairstyle. Cher has her rocker glam style. Jennifer Aniston has her fresh clean American modern style. Kim Kardashian aims for sexy glamour. You get the point.

Every woman needs to define her look and change that when it no longer works for her. Your fashion type can change over the years, as you change and evolve.

Some of the women look perplexed. *"Okay, let's take out some fashion magazines. Circle the things that resonate to you and let's find how many fashion types you like. Remember this is for you to wear and all about you. No one else! Don't think about 'who will like me in this.' Just think how you will like you in this outfit. Feel if your energy goes up or down when you see it. Be selective and go within."*

After about thirty minutes, I ask people to stand up and talk about their fashion types and show us examples from their magazines. Most of my students know what they like when they see it. Some people have worn the same look for way too long, only because they were afraid to try something new. I encourage everyone to find the right look to help them reach his or her life goals: more success, better relationships, more sizzle in their sex lives, etc.

A few of the women shout out, "Eve, what is your fashion type?"

"Mine? I love a mix of modern, trendy, and dramatic with a sexy, edgy and feminine flair. What I don't do is serious conservative. No, that doesn't work for me. I must always wear sexy high fashion shoes. That's non-negotiable. I love clothing that makes my heart skip a beat like a gorgeous Italian man that gives you the chills just to look at him!" I say with a big smile and a sway of my hips. Everyone gets a good laugh out of this. In other words, I know what works for me and I've created my own style.

I ask for a volunteer. Many hands shoot up. I scan the room to see who would make a good example of everything we have learned about having a great image.

"Okay. Ruth. Would you kindly be our model? Great, please come up to the front of the room with me," I say, as Ruth jumps up. *"Everyone, all eyes on Ruth. Ruth, is your coloring cool or warm?"*

Ruth says, "I have cool coloring. I am a Winter."

"Very good. Yes, you are a Winter. What is your contrast level?"

"Contrasting," she says.

"Why?" I ask.

"Because I have dark hair, light skin and dark blue eyes" Ruth answers.

"Perfect! Now, Ruth, please do not answer this next question," I implore. *"Everyone, what is Ruth's inner line? Curved or angular?"* I ask as I look around the room.

"Angular!" a few people shout.

"Ruth, is that correct?"

"Yes, I have a diamond shaped face."

"Fabulous! That's correct! Next, what is your outer line? Curved, curvilinear or linear?" I demand.

"It is linear. I don't really have a waist. I never did."

"Where do you carry your weight?" I want to know.

"All around my middle and on my upper hips. I have high square hips" she says.

"And what is your slimmest area?" I ask.

"My legs. Oh, and I have a flat butt. That really bothers me. I hate it." Ruth admits.

"So what area of your body would you want to accentuate?" I inquire.

"My chest, bustline and legs."

"And which areas do you want to camouflage?"

"I don't want people to notice my tummy, back fat, and flat rear end!" Ruth says emphatically.

"Okay. Now we need to know what kind of natural texture you have?"

"I am smooth with a little bit of texture in my hair if I don't flatiron it. I love smooth fabrics the best."

"And last, what is your fashion type? What kinds of styles express the real you?"

"Modern, elegant, feminine and classic. Is that okay to be a mix?"

To which I say, "Yes, that's great. And easy to find in the stores."

Everyone is amazed at how the pieces of this puzzle they just learned are beginning to fit together. Finally! I can see from their eyes and their enthusiasm that this is starting to make sense.

"Okay, let's analyze what Ruth is wearing today and if it is flattering her or not. Then let's talk about why, using the What Makes Me Special information we just learned. Ready?"

"Ruth is a Winter. Is she wearing colors that flatter her or not?" I ask.

"Yes and no, I think," shouts Susan.

"Her lace jacket is gold, which seems to drain her coloring and is more of an Autumn gold. But her necklace, skirt, and shoes are black which is great for a Winter."

"The jacket color is not great," says Susan.

Then another student says, "I thought some Winters can wear gold."

"Oh, you ladies are so smart! Yes, some Winters can wear gold if they have Mediterranean ethnicity in them or if they have olive eyes or cool hazel eyes or gold in their hair. But Ruth has clear blue eyes and she is the kind of Winter that really needs to stay with her colors and not venture out from them. She looks best in cool metallics such as silver, white gold and platinum. Yellow gold doesn't bring out the best in her and should be avoided," I instruct. "What about Ruth's hair color? Is it the best brown for her?" I ask.

"Not really. It's okay, but not fabulous," answers a group of the ladies.

"Because it's kind of mousey, not dramatic enough for her coloring?" they shout out.

"What would be better?" I prod.

"Darker brown or black?"

"Wow! I am impressed. You are spot on! What about Ruth's makeup and nail color? Is it good?"

"We like her deep red lipstick and nail polish. But her eye makeup could be more dramatic," they explain to me.

"Yes! My thoughts exactly!" I say.

"Ruth, do these comments seem accurate?"

Ruth nods yes.

"May I touch up your hair and makeup?" I ask. "Please come sit in the director's chair."

I add some black eyeliner to her gorgeous eyes to accentuate them and make them more dramatic. Then I pull out a flatiron to smooth her hair, which instantly makes it appear darker. "Does this bring her energy and power up or down?" I ask everyone.

"UP!! Way up! Wow, those little things made such a difference!" All the women shout and gather around in amazement.

"Now, what about Ruth's neckline choices? Does her necklace and shape of her jacket neckline flatter her or not?"

"The jacket is collarless and has a round neckline. It fights her facial shape and ages her ... rounds out her dramatic angular facial shape." Tina says.

"Very observant. What neckline would be more flattering?" I ask.

"A V-neck or a Forties style sweetheart neckline in cobalt blue or bright red." someone answers.

"And her bold black necklace?" I ask.

"It is made of diamond shapes but it doesn't thrill me on her. The total shape is too round. But I'm not sure what would make it better," Susan says.

"Like her neckline, it needs to angle or point more at the bottom. She needs the shape to be more edgy and dramatic like her facial shape and essence," I teach. Then I put my finger at the bottom of her necklace and gently pull it down creating more of an angled v-shape. "Do you all see the difference? Now watch."

I have Ruth unbutton a couple of the top buttons of her lace jacket. Then I fold the fabric in, to create more of a V-neck. "Did you all just see what happened to her energy and her face, just by mimicking her inner line?"

"Oh my God, that's amazing!! Her face just lit up!" they all say.

I drape a piece of cobalt blue fabric over her jacket so the right color is next to her face. The color repeats her intense blue eyes. Everyone screams at how incredible Ruth looks with these few modifications.

"Great group! I am impressed. Ruth, did you feel fabulous in your necklace and lace jacket the way it was?" I say as I look her in the eyes.

"No, not fabulous. I thought they were classy and elegant, and the price was right. But I don't wear them much, because no, I don't feel great in them. But I never knew why before and I felt badly not wearing them more because they were so expensive," Ruth admits.

"Oh! So expensive doesn't guarantee that you'll look great and love what you bought?" I shout. "Ruth, do you like your necklace and jacket more now?"

"Oh, yes! I can really see and feel a difference. I feel much more beautiful and sexy. And I don't feel as thick waisted because you brought much more attention to my face and bustline. I love that."

"Listen up everyone. For very little time and money, Ruth can correct her wardrobe. She can have her jacket neckline changed into a v-neck, at a depth that flatters her face and décolleté. She can go to the bead store and find an angled pendant to add to her beautiful black necklace. And she can buy a low cut cobalt blue camisole to peep out from under her jacket."

"Eve, shouldn't Ruth give away or sell that gold jacket as it's not her best color?"

"She could. But I would prefer she wears her hair and makeup in the correct colors and style, correct her necklace, add the camisole (all pieces she can wear with other things) and enjoy the investment she made ... which will boost her self-esteem and get her mileage out of her investment. However, yes, in the future, Ruth would be best to avoid that gold color," I confirm.

"You see, the point of learning What Makes You Special and all that I am teaching you, is not for you all to feel badly about what you already own and throw it away. No, not at all. The point is to raise your awareness and help you wear what you have more effectively and in the future to shop correctly … thus avoiding these painful and costly mistakes." I say as I walk around the room.

"Let's go back to Ruth. We appreciate your letting us learn with you as our model." I tell her. "Let's talk about 'accentuating and camouflaging' your body proportions and features. As we know, Ruth said she doesn't like her tummy, high hips and flat rear end. Right, Ruth?"

She nods in agreement.

"Now let's look at her outfit to see what she chose to accentuate. Her jacket is way lighter than her long black slim skirt. Is it not? We have learned that light brings out and dark recedes. Therefore, isn't her light gold jacket accentuating her upper torso width? And isn't the lacey pattern adding weight to her midriff?"

"Yeah! Wow!" Everyone yells out.

"Now look at where the bottom of her jacket hits … right at her widest part, the top of her square high hips. So our eyes go directly to what Ruth wants to camouflage. Can you all see that?" Everyone gathers around as they are so amazed they can't stay in their seats.

"Ruth, please turn around. Everyone, please notice that her slim thin jersey skirt makes Ruth's rear end appear smaller and flatter. Didn't Ruth tell us that she doesn't like how flat her rear end is?" I tell them as I look around.

"Wouldn't it have been better for Ruth to have worn a skirt made of a thicker fabric that has seams, pleats or pockets on the rear end to add fullness and curves? Better than that, all she had to do was buy a jacket that is longer, hitting at the middle of her rear that flares out in the back, has pleats or fullness below the waist to create the illusion of a fuller rear, while drawing our eyes away from her midriff and upper hips. Can you all understand how that would have been a wiser choice for her goals?" I have always believed that knowledge and awareness are the keys to lasting personal power.

I am thrilled. I am high on the excitement of teaching this material that has taken me a lifetime to learn. I wish I could have taught these skills to my own mother, to heal her, but I know now that would have been impossible. My mother's illness gave me the gift of loving and appreciating beauty and the power it holds for every person willing to express it.

CHAPTER EIGHT

How to Shop, Follow Trends and Get the Most from Your Wardrobe

YOUR CLOSET TALKS

"Okay, everyone! Are you ready to clean out your closets? Are you ready to let go of the mess, guilt and the shame? Are you ready to let go of the mistakes and the dust?"

Closets say a lot about a person. For years, as an image consultant, one of the services I offer is to help my clients clean out, organize and beautify their closets. I always found it fascinating. Their closets always speak volumes about their discipline, self-esteem, self-love, and self-worth. It also speaks volumes about their priorities and their organizational skills. Over time I came to see that it's almost impossible to be well-dressed if your closet is a mess. Like everything else I teach about, beautiful closets create a beautiful state of mind for the person who owns them. By now, you must realize that I think beauty needs to be created everywhere we exist! I recall the saying that "how we do anything is how we do everything."

Think about it. If you walk into your closet and it is a dusty, dirty, unorganized mess … what subliminal message does that say to you about all the time, money and effort you put into buying those clothes? Does it reek of success or failure? Does it uplift your spirits or make you feel disgusted? The mess looms in your subconscious as another big failure you must someday attend to. Not a great way to start your day, in my opinion. About fifteen years ago, I listened to a Jack Canfield tape about success and organization. He said that the first thing he does when coaching clients for success is to make them organize their entire homes and offices. Jack taught that our subconscious minds can only hold 100 attention flags before our mind goes on overload from these "flags" which then hampers our ability to do our best. I always remember that when I want to put off organizing things. Most closets account for a huge amount of attention flags. Coincidentally, most people hate the prospect of cleaning their closets, but feel elated once they actually do.

How could something so seemingly trivial as organizing a closet be so important? The answer is simple. When we organize what we have in a way that makes it easier to use and when we give away what no longer serves us to someone in need, we feel a surge of positive energy. Simply stated, we feel freer, lighter, and more in control. The sense of accomplishment is fantastic!

Get your egos out of your closet! We all have too many emotions invested in our wardrobes and unfortunately they are mostly negative. Based on the fact that most Americans wear only 10–20% of their clothing, there are a lot of mistakes hanging in our closets, collecting dust. Let's put our egos in the parking lot once again, so we can let go of our emotional attachments to the clothing that are literally hanging us up and preventing us from moving forward in this process. All puns are intended!

The idea of cleaning your closet is to get rid of everything that doesn't represent who you really are. Be mindful that "who you are" changes over time and the content of your closet needs to reflect those changes. In other words, our wardrobe must evolve as we evolve. You may have a different career, new hobbies, and new social activities that require modifications to your wardrobe. If you can look at your closet from this perspective you will see that your wardrobe is not static, as it is ever changing to meet your needs. With your new knowledge about what makes you special, you will be able to separate your ego from your wardrobe and make wiser decisions about what you buy, what you keep and what you wear.

CLOSET ORGANIZATION

Most Americans have a lot more clothing than they will ever wear. There is a huge focus on "quantity" not "quality and fit" in this country. In Europe, for example, people have very small closets, but they are usually much more stylish and well-dressed than we are. There is a great emphasis on quality and fit. The focus is on the right clothing, not huge amounts of "whatever we got on sale" kind of clothing. Europeans covet classic clothing and accessories that add value to their wardrobe and class to their image. It is a different mindset.

It's essential that our closets contain the right things that are in alignment with all the principles of our color harmony, inner line, outer line, etc. Our closets need to be clean, neat and organized. Everything should be easy to access and as visible as possible. Proper hangers are important to keep the shape of our clothing intact. Visually, it's better if our hangers match and if our closets have special movable shelves, chrome rods and cabinets. Closet organizing companies can help maximize the space and efficiency of our closets and are well worth the expense. Home Depot, The Container Stores, and Lowe's all have "do it yourself" closet organizing departments which will save a lot of money and can produce a similar result. But most importantly, you have to realize the importance of having an organized, aesthetically pleasing, clean closet that helps make getting dressed each day easier.

How we treat our closets is a reflection of how we feel about our appearance. Do you look at your clothing as an afterthought or is it something just to cover your nudity and protect you from the elements? Is your clothing an expression of your inner self, your attributes, your expertise, and your talents? Does your clothing command power and self-respect and heighten your self-esteem or does it make you feel embarrassed or less than who you are? I would encourage all of you to ask the same questions about your closets. After all, they house this big investment called your wardrobe and it deserves your respect and attention.

I can't help but flash back to when I was training to become a certified image consultant. My teacher came to my house to organize and audit my closet. I vividly remember how harsh she was about my so-called "mistakes." I can still feel my hands cross tightly over my stomach defensively and how upset I felt. All of my mistakes seemed to jump out at me and I felt so ashamed over the money I had wasted. I felt horrible and for a moment regretted ever having that woman in my closet; I learned something invaluable. I learned how emotionally charged our wardrobes are, right or wrong. I also decided in that moment that I would never make a client of mine feel ashamed of her mistakes if I could help it. I vowed to find another way to help people with their wardrobes and how to effectively toss out that "walk in closet, walk of shame."

I am often asked by my students, "How often should we organize our closets?"

At least twice a year: spring and fall, to prepare for the different seasons, weather and activities. More often if you like. But twice a year your closet needs a complete cleaning and re-organizing. At first, this may be a painful process and you may need someone to help you get through it. But over time, you will be able to be objective and approach your closet as you would an important piece of real estate for which you are paying rent or a monthly mortgage. Yes, that's correct. You pay a price for every square foot of your closet, so it had better be worthwhile to maximize the investment!

I began my television career on Christina Ferrare's Home and Family Show. Christina confessed that she had a really difficult time letting go of old pieces of clothing that had strong memories attached to them, even if she was no longer wearing them. She did a segment about that issue on air. She said that someone once advised her to create a "memory box" to store those special pieces. I thought that was a great idea. Many of you may want to purchase a beautiful storage box for this purpose. Fold any memorable clothing, shoes or accessories and put them away in that box. Put the box way up high on a shelf, in a storage room or in your garage. Anywhere it will be protected. Just knowing you have these things will bring you comfort and doing this will free up space for the things you really wear. Here are the guidelines for your closet organizing:

- Physically clean, dust, and vacuum the entire closet … every nook and cranny.
- Use proper hangers. Nothing should be left on dry-cleaning wire hangers as they warp and deform the shape of the shoulder line of your garments.
- Nothing should be stored in dry cleaning bags. Your clothes need to breathe.
- Everything must be properly hung on the right type of hanger; example, pants on an appropriate pant hanger.
- Knits and sweaters are best folded, not hung to keep their shape.
- Use cedar shoe trees to preserve the shape of your shoes and take moisture out.
- Use natural lavender sachets to repel moths.
- Use shoulder covers to keep items you don't wear often, dust free.

We are ready to begin sorting through our imaginary closet. I want you to create four sections:

The *give away with joy* pile.
The *needs alterations* pile.
The *needs something to wear with it* pile.
The *keep it* pile.

Ask yourself the following questions about each and every item in your closet while auditing it:

- Is it my color, or one of my flow colors?
- Is it my correct inner line?
- Is it my correct Outer Line?
- Does it accentuate the areas of my body I want to draw attention to?
- Does the fabric feel good to me and compliment my natural texture level?
- Does it flatter my figure?
- Is it well made?
- Has it been more than two years since I've worn it? If so, why?

Also, ask yourself about each item:

- How does this item make me look?
- Does this communicate the person I am today?
- What message does this send about me?
- How does this make me feel?
- Do I really enjoy wearing it?
- Does my vibration/energy go up or down when I wear it?

There are many ways to organize your clothing:

- **Shades.** Light to dark, such as all blouses or shirts hung on one rack in order of whites to blacks.
- **Sections.** Some like to hang all their outfits for work in one area. Other people like to categorize by activity: work clothes, weekend clothes, special occasion clothes, etc. However you choose to organize

your closet by section, putting like colors together makes things easier.
- **Shoes.** Shoes are best stored in clear shoes boxes or on specially made shoes shelves.
- **Belts, ties, and long necklaces.** Investigate pull out racks to see if they fit your closet... There are scarf rings to hang your scarves or clear stackable boxes for folding them.
- **Be Creative.** Some people paint their closets in a favorite color. Others make them luxurious with custom made all wood shelves and cabinets. However you decide to decorate and design your closet is up to you. I encourage all of you to put a lot of love, time, and as much money as you comfortably can into making your closet a place you adore.

Congratulations! After you have audited and cleaned out your closet you are almost ready to shop. In order to avoid more mistakes, I want you all to study the new trends of the season. Decide which ones are viable options for you based on your fashion type, career, personality, and taste level. You can do this by reading fashion magazines, looking online at fashion websites, and paying attention to clothing store displays. You will see definite major trends and then you can decide which ones to follow. Never, ever wear a trend if it doesn't look good on you or make you feel great. I don't want you to be a fashion victim. You also need to use your good judgment to be discerning about which trend to wear and how much of it.

TRENDS

Trends are like a bell curve. In my bootcamp class I use a flip chart to demonstrate this point. On the left side of the bell curve, down low, we see the haute couture fashions. These are the newest styles that cost about $30,000 and up, per outfit. They are made to order and are very new, different, and sometimes shocking. As we move up the bell curve, maybe six months later more designers are creating the same trend and making it more affordable. At this stage, a similar kind of outfit costs about $5,000–$15,000 and can be found at high-end department stores and boutiques, in very limited quantities. More time elapses and now we find this trend in the $1,000–$5,000 price range in larger quantities and in more stores. We are almost at the top of the bell curve now. As the prices go down and the inventories of this trend go up, we see it coming down the right side of the bell curve. At the end of the bell curve, this trend is offered everywhere, at every price point in huge quantities.

Trends used to take 5–7 years to complete their cycle from first glimpse introduction to being mass marketed. Nowadays, the cycle is much faster … taking only two years (or less) to be offered at the low end price point. However, I still believe that to reach the masses, it takes a good 3–5 years for what I call integration, which in my mind is where people from all walks of life are wearing a certain trend. For example, for years now we have all been wearing flat front lower rise pants and jeans. Two years ago I saw glimpses of the high rise, pleated and wide legged trouser coming off the haute couture runway. I also know, from experience, that the fashion pendulum must go from one extreme to the other in order to keep us moving forward and to keep us buying more clothing. The low rise, slim legged pant was tapped out. How many pairs can each person own? So it was only logical that the other extreme would start to make a resurgence.

It will probably take a full four to five years for this new high-waisted, wide-legged trouser with optional pleats to be in every person's wardrobe. My point with all of this is that you have to know where to catch the wave … a.k.a. the fashion trend wave. Do you pay more and get a full five years or more out of the trend? Or do you wait, play it safe, and buy it when you're certain it's acceptable, risking wearing it only 1–2 years? The other consideration is how do you want to be seen? As a fashion leader? As a modernist? Or as more conservative and safe? Where is your comfort zone and what is important to you? Where is your comfort level and how far are you willing to stretch out of it? Only you will know by experimenting within the limits of your fashion zone.

I would bet that many of you feel that you never have anything new to wear because you wait to incorporate a trend so late on the bell curve that it is already on the way out so you never look modern or in style.

It is the same scenario for men and women. The only difference is that men's trends change more slowly and less often. But they do change and evolve none the less and men need to stay on top of trends too or they will risk looking stale and out of style.

People who are fashion leaders are the ones who pick up the trends as soon as they can. They want to wear the newest and be the first. Doing that takes tremendous confidence and lots of money. The masses may not appreciate your cutting edge sense of style. They may scratch their heads and wonder what the heck you have on, when it's a new trend. This won't work for everyone or every career. What you need to take responsibility for is deciding when to add a trend, which trend of the variety out there to add, and decipher which trends will send the right message about you. Always go back to the fact that image is communication. Therefore if image is communication, then trends are the punctuation marks that add excitement and flair to your message. How much or how little you punctuate your appearance is up to you. However, always remember that no punctuation, as in language, leaves room for misinterpretation and doubt. So we can not afford to ignore trends in fashion.

Please note that the faster the world changes due to technology, the faster the trends change. Therefore, in today's world, it's better to buy less and buy more often to keep yourself current. Think about how televisions, computers and cell phones improve every year. You want to take advantage of the newest and the best. The same holds true for your image. It needs to also be fresh and new. In the way medical science is finding ways to keep us young and vibrant, there is no room for us to look old and used. This whole new way of aging is demanding an entire new way of dressing. Keeping your pulse on the trends is a sure fired way to do that. The choice then is up to you, once again, for how you are perceived.

COST PER WEARING

Now that you understand more clearly, the importance of incorporating trends into your wardrobe, let's discuss the economic side of your wardrobe investment. It's called the cost per wearing formula. This is extremely important for those of you wanting to elevate your consciousness from quantity to quality purchasing. Doing this requires a paradigm shift that takes some effort. To help you with that often emotional shift, the "cost per wearing" formula will help you see things more clearly. For example, if you wear denims four days a week, on average, then you would want to pay a higher price for your denims as they are a core piece of your wardrobe. Therefore, even if you pay $200 for a pair, it may be a very low cost per wearing. The formula would be four times a week multiplied by fifty-two weeks in a year would be 208 wearings per year: then divide the $200 investment by 208 wearings, which ends up costing you $.96 per wearing. Now, most people wear their denims about 2 years. Divided again, the cost per wearing goes to less than $.48 per wearing.

Compare this to a pair of denims that cost you $75, but they don't fit great and aren't that comfortable. So you end up wearing them about once a month, if that. The cost per wearing now becomes $6.25 per wearing. Another example that will really drive this concept home is buying an evening gown. A beautiful cocktail dress that costs $500 but is worn only one to two times a year, ends up costing you $250 per wearing. If you wear it for two years, the cost goes to $125 per wearing. I'm certain you get the point. Perhaps for your career or your social life, you need to spend a lot of money for a cocktail dress or for an evening suit. If so, do it gladly. However, if you are on a budget, then shop the discounters and sales to find an elegant evening ensemble for way less than normal retail and put your money into items that you will wear a lot.

The other way to put your money into good cost per wearing items is to buy items that transition from day to evening. This is where you can get the best cost per wearing of all.

I was recently asked by a long distance private client to dress her, for two galas she was going to attend for her work. As she has a high powered job, she was willing to spend up to $5,000 on her dress. Instead, I found her a fabulous designer dress for $1,200 that we dressed up with long gloves, designer stiletto high heeled pumps, and gorgeous jewelry. As I kept her accessories black, she was able to use an evening bag she already owned. She also had an evening wrap we bought five years ago that was perfect to wear over the dress.

My client can now wear this dress for ten years or more. She can top it with a blazer for work or a cashmere cardigan for more casual work. She can change the same belt to a leather one for a totally different look. She can dress down by wearing knee high or ankle boots with the dress. She can wear opaque tights to winterize the dress. And she can layer this print dress with another print to pull off the very new print mix look. Because she can wear this dress for so long and in so many ways, this is a fabulous value. And that's how we have to think when we invest in our wardrobes. Because it is an investment!!

Men are thrilled to learn this concept too. For years I would encourage my male clients to buy what Europeans call soft suits. What this means is that the suit shoulder line is softer and more relaxed, lending itself to a transitional look;

not just a dressy or corporate look. When men buy these kinds of suits, they get a much better cost per wearing; they can wear the suit with a dressier t-shirt, polo shirt, or a nice shirt that looks good without a tie. Transitioning the soft suit from nice casual to corporate or dressy is just a matter of the shirting underneath and the choice of belt/shoes. This is also an amazing style of suit for travel as the jacket can be worn with denims, the slacks with various shirts and sweaters or together as a suit for dressier occasions. Again, it's buying clothing that has great versatility, wonderful tailoring, and good quality that will take you far in life and always represent you well. Quality really does make a huge difference.

Clothing that costs you more, can actually cost you less to wear. That's the quantity into quality paradigm or mindset. And by the way, you can buy quality items at a huge discount if you know what you're doing. To learn more about quality fabrics and construction, go to higher end stores. Really look at the merchandise from the inside, out. Ask the sales associates to explain why the garment costs what it does. Look, touch, and feel the clothing. Get acquainted with luxury garments and luxury prices. Get to know the designers that fit you best and whose designs resonate to you. Go to fabric stores. Feel the expensive fabrics then feel the cheapest ones. Note the difference. In order to be a savvy shopper and be able to buy luxury goods at a discount, you must train your eyes and your fingertips.

For years, I have been taking my clients and students on resale designer consignment shopping tours. They learn to buy luxury goods at ten to thirty cents on the dollar! They are always amazed how I know which items are a great deal and which are not. That is because I am familiar with the designers, their normal prices, and which year the item was made (for the most part). Therefore, I can spot a designer coat that normally costs $1,500 and is now at the resale shop for a fantastic buy at $150! I also know when I go to the discount stores, which of their items are what I call loss leaders. Loss leaders are high quality items that draw the savvy shoppers to the store, but the rest of the merchandise is of lesser quality. I know good construction and fabric, I can see the really good buys. Seven years ago, I bought my husband two shirts from H & M in New York. He stills gets compliments on those shirts and they still look like new. They are equal to his $100 shirts in fabric and construction. He still marvels over how much use he has gotten from them. My husband loves good quality fashion!

Shopping is an art and a science. You learned the science of it today. Now we will pull all of the information together so you can use your creativity for the art of dressing well. It is not as daunting or difficult as it seems. In fact, it's fabulously fun! Here we go ...

CHAPTER NINE

The Smart Shopper's Guide to Investing in Your Wardrobe Portfolio

Knowing how to shop well is important for many reasons. The most important reason is that our wardrobes are the tools of our visual communication (as are our hair, makeup and grooming). Because of this, our wardrobes require constant updating and editing. Most people understand they need to do this with their computers, telephones and other electronic devices; however they don't want to acknowledge that their wardrobes also require constant refreshing. The other reason is it's less stressful and a lot more effective to know what you're doing. Clothing costs too much money to leave your shopping expertise to chance.

Trendy wardrobes require more work, classic wardrobes less. It's important to understand, however, that ALL styles of wardrobes require adding trends seasonally, even if only a few. Without the modern panache of trends, a wardrobe gets outmoded fast! Just like people look foolish using a clunky thick cell phone from five years ago, their clothing looks foolish too if they ignore the current trends and refuse to modernize.

The other day I was interviewing a trend and marketing expert on my radio show. I asked her point blank, "Why is it that Americans buy much more quantity than quality?"

To which she replied, "That's because Americans are consumers with a consumer mentality."

To me this is evident in our approach to clothing and food: fast, cheap and lots of it! It's high time that we started realizing that this isn't serving either our health or our pocketbooks.

I understand and value the importance of retail therapy, as we female shopaholics like to call our sport shopping habit. Truthfully, any purchase is an investment, and as such needs to be taken seriously and strategized. What you buy needs to make sense and augment your wardrobe. When you get good at shopping, you can shop for fun and do something good for yourself and those you love. First, you have to know what you're doing. Shopping effectively is a skill that should be taught in school. Since it is not, you need to take this seriously.

Imagine an average American woman has $1000 to spend. She will run out without much thought and see how many pieces of clothing she can buy for that money. She may buy a bunch of shoes and some accessories, but the main focus is on how much and how fast. If her significant other is lucky, she may buy a couple of pairs of cheap panties. After shopping, she can't wait to call her best friend and tell her how many things she bought for her $1000; how many bags of stuff she got!

Never mind that 80% or more will probably hardly get used (and will sit and collect dust). Never mind that most of it is poorly made, doesn't flatter her, doesn't fit the way it should, is in the wrong color, and the fabric doesn't feel right. Regardless, she justifies buying what she did because of sentiments like, "Isn't this just too cute? I just had to have it!!"

I call this "Unconscious Shopping!" For the most part, Americans shop unconsciously, unaware of how they are throwing away their hard earned money and buying clothing that may actually hinder their chances of success rather than help them. It is a case of immediate gratification that doesn't yield long-term results. And since most of it is never worn and enjoyed, it just sits in the closet taking up space ... making the person feel more like a failure over time than a winner.

My husband and I often wonder who is buying all these clothes, since we hardly ever see people dressing nicely anymore. It's like the infamous American diet industry. We spend more on diet aids, low fat food, and weight reduction than any other country in the world and yet we keep on getting fatter. We buy food much the same way we buy clothes; quantity, not quality and it's making us obese and sick. Our shopping patterns are making our images look sick and slovenly, and helping us go into needless debt. Time to wake up!

Now let's talk about how the average European woman shops with that same $1000. She may visit ten to twenty boutiques (or more) to find the one or two items that she can add to her wardrobe. She considers each item she adds to her wardrobe as an investment and takes the process very seriously. She will take her time to find the right thing because she knows that she will wear it for years. It will be the finest item she can find for the $750 out of her $1,000 that she has to spend and it will be exquisitely made and fit her beautifully. If it needs some alterations, she will take it to her coveted seamstress. She strives to buy designer brands if she can afford it. Yes, the European woman takes pride in being able to buy the finest quality. It's a very different paradigm and it's working well, considering that the average European has about a tenth of the clothing most Americans have and they look way more stylish and elegant. Quantity obviously isn't the answer.

You may be wondering what she will do with the remaining $250 left over. She will buy some exquisitely made lingerie: a bra and one or two pair of panties, or a negligee. She does this because she understands the importance of what is under her clothing. Her foundations make everything look better. She treasures her lingerie and knows what it does for her feminine sensuality. It is never, ever an afterthought and she knows its worth.

The way we shop in this country is indicative of our overall attitude about life. We don't savor it. We want instant gratification. We don't want to take time and effort to get it right. We work day and night and feel guilty to take a one-week vacation so we can buy a bunch of things we don't need and that don't look good on us. We do this at the expense of our health and our families. We are paying the price. We need to have balance and take the time to spend with our families, take time to dine instead of shoving food in our mouths, and we need to take time to vacation for three to four weeks a year like the rest of the world does. Think about it. If our current way of life is working, then why are we in the state we're in?

Let's start changing our paradigm of shopping by learning a new way to shop. We are going to go on an imaginary shopping excursion. We are not going to think about price. Yes, you heard me! Price is the last thing we look at when shopping because focusing on price has gotten us into this mess. Focusing on other elements will change how we shop. I also want you all to think about your company's dress code and if they don't have one, create your own personal dress code. This will help you raise your personal standards when you go to shop. Hold yourself accountable for how you present yourself and keep that in the forefront of your mind when you enter a store.

SHOPPING ORDER OF IMPORTANCE

I want everyone to make a copy of this list to carry in your wallet until you memorize the sequence. Never forget that Image = Power. By learning to shop properly, you are taking back your power and creating a powerful image. Here are the steps:

- Color
- Fabric
- Inner Line
- Outer Line
- Construction/Quality
- Fit
- How the item makes you feel
- What message it sends
- Is it your fashion type?
- Price (consider cost per wearing when looking at price)

I am now going to walk you all through an imaginary shopping excursion so that we can learn how to use my ten steps. Today we are going to pretend that we are all looking for a new blazer to wear to work. Select a department store where you are comfortable shopping and that you think carries merchandise in your price range. Do not think about money. Stay focused on learning the right way to shop. I want you to shop alone. You can ask a salesperson for assistance in finding the right item, but may not rely on them to make your selections.

The reason you need to shop alone until you learn how to shop is that you need to learn how to resonate to what works best for your unique shape and coloring. This is something you must learn to feel without outside influences. If you shop with a friend or family member, they will offer their opinions, which can confuse you. They will also usually suggest that you buy colors, shapes and styles that they like or look good on them. I'm not joking. For years when I would audit a client's closet I could always tell, for example, which ties a man's wife picked out because they were all in her season and inner line, not his. So while you are learning, shop on your own. When you do shop with someone else later on, don't stray from what you know looks good on you.

COLOR

As you enter the store, you go to the career wear department and start scanning the area for blazers. You are going to look for color first. You are going to find a color that flatters you and is right for your seasonal color harmony. If it's not your color, it's of no use to you. So look for the best color you can find that makes you glow and look healthy. If the color doesn't flatter you, it may make you look sick or anemic; therefore, pay attention to finding the right shade and take the time to do that. If the store has fluorescent lighting, walk to a window or door to look at the color more closely. If you're shopping at night, make certain the item is refundable so you can check the color in natural daylight before you are committed to keeping it.

FABRIC

Next thing you will consider is the fabric. You need to touch it, feel it and see how you resonate to the hand of the fabric. The hand is the weight and feel of a fabric. If you are a smooth textured person, then find silky, soft, supple fabrics. If you have a lot of texture to your skin and hair, look for fabrics that have texture, embroidery, pleats, and are not as smooth. Remember, if it doesn't match your texture levels and feel good to your skin, you won't ever like wearing it.

INNER LINE

Once you know you like the fabric and it resonates to you in feel and comfort, you need to look at the garment's Inner Line. Is it angular or curved? It should match your own Inner Line. Check out the lapel shape, pockets, buttons and pattern (if not solid) to see if they match your Inner Line. If they don't, then keep looking. This applies to any other piece of clothing that you consider wearing.

OUTER LINE

Next, check the Outer Line of the blazer. It needs to flatter your body shape. If you have a curved (hourglass) Outer Line (bone structure), then the Outer

Line of your blazer must also be curved. It must have a definite waistline: curved in shape, belted at the waist, or a peplum design. This applies to any of the three Outer Line shapes; that is … no waist with straight Outer Line, some waistline emphasis with a curvilinear Outer Line.

CONSTRUCTION AND QUALITY

The fifth element to consider is the construction and quality. Open the jacket. See how it's made. How are buttons sewn on? Are the buttonholes sewn well or are they puckered and are the threads coming undone? How are the seams? Do they lie flat or do they pull in some areas unevenly? What about the lining? Is it silk or some other fine fabric? Does it look as beautiful on the inside as the outside? If so, chances are there was pride and good workmanship put into that garment. You can tell more about the construction and quality after you try on the garment and see how it fits on your body.

Now you are ready to try the garments on in the fitting room. Think of this part as the process of elimination. Know that you will have a high chance of success by the time you go into the fitting room if you have followed this process. It's very helpful to get to know the fit of the different designers' clothing lines that you like. Each designer follows a certain cut and pattern. Their clothing is called their line. Some lines run small, some true to size and some generous. Lines that always run a size big are said to have "vanity sizing." If you remember how each line runs, you will know what size to bring into the fitting room.

As you are trying on your selections, make certain there is a three way mirror in the dressing room or that you have a small hand held mirror with you. It's crucial that you view how you look in a piece of clothing from all angles: frontal, side profile and rear view. Notice how the garment drapes on your body. Does the collar hug your neck like an ass on a saddle? When you button the blazer, does the chest area lie flat to your chest or does it pull open? Does the shoulder seam line up to your shoulder? What about the back vents (if there are any)? Do they lay flat? Most garments can be taken in more easily than they can be let out. For a jacket, the collar, chest and throw of the neck cannot be altered successfully, but you can shorten the sleeves and lengthen them in some cases. Waist and hip areas can be taken in. Be careful because not all fabrics can be let out without leaving sewing marks. Know what can or can't be done with alterations. The best rule of thumb is to fit your largest or widest part and tailor down the rest. For example, if your bust line (or for a man, the chest) is your widest part, then buy a jacket that fits comfortably on that area and have the rest of the jacket taken in to fit your slimmer areas like your waist and hips.

Now that you know the blazer fits you well and meets all your unique criteria, I want you to get silent and look at yourself in the mirror. I mean really look, not just see. Notice how this blazer makes you feel and think about where you want to wear it. Is it for work? If so, does it make you feel more successful and powerful? If it is for social occasions, does it make you feel sexy and alluring? Every piece of clothing has a vibration, an energy of its own. It's up to you to notice what happens to your energy when you put that piece of clothing on your body. Ask yourself if your energy just went up or down. Do this alone. Don't have anyone in the fitting room with you while you decide whether to buy the item or not. If you feel a surge of positive energy, then move on to the next step.

You need to think about the message this blazer sends. It is power? Success? Vibrancy? Competency? Sexiness? Trustworthiness? Trendiness? Conservativeness? What is the message? Is it sending the message you need it to send? This is crucial. If you want to look mature and competent, then you don't want to buy a blazer that makes you look sexy and edgy. It won't be speaking the language you need it to speak.

The next to last thing to consider is if this blazer is your fashion type or someone else's. Do you like preppy and this blazer is rocker? Or are you a feminine dramatic type and this blazer is conservative? You and your clothing need to be a fashion type match or you'll never feel right wearing it. Of course, your type may change and evolve over the years, but you are shopping in the moment. So at this moment what is your type? You need to really know that and be honest with yourself. Even if you admire someone else's fashion type or savvy, be truthful with yourself as to your needs and comfort zone. If you've done your homework, you will understand what you like.

The very last thing to consider is the price! After the jacket meets all of your needs, look at the price. Now ask yourself how often you think you will wear this blazer. Is it a year round fabric? Can you dress it up or down? Can you wear it with many different pieces of clothing that you already own? Go back to your cost per wearing formula. You may find that it's worth spending more because it will actually cost you less over the life of the garment. Also, ask yourself what this blazer will do to help you be more successful. Then you will be able to determine if it's worth the price. Your answer may surprise you as you now look at your clothing purchases in a new, more educated light.

The last glitch that is preventing you all from shopping effectively is your feelings of lack. Yes, that's correct. Your feelings of lack and all the negative feelings you have attached to spending money on yourself. Almost every person I have ever met wants to make more money and wants to be wealthy; yet, almost every client I have ever had is afraid or intimidated to shop in expensive high-end stores. If you believe in the Law of Attraction, how can you attract wealth when you are afraid to shop where wealthy people shop? You can not attract what you repel.

Here is what I did to change my own wealth consciousness. I learned this exercise from the teachings of Abraham by Esther and Jerry Hicks in their book *The Law of Attraction* and their other writings. They teach about going shopping with $100 (real or imaginary) in your wallet. You go into a nice store and play the "pretend shopping game." You go in feeling good about what you are planning to buy that day and pretend you are spending that $100. I learned this concept from them over twenty years ago, but with inflation, I have changed the amount to $1,000. For myself, I decided to try it with an imaginary $10,000 shopping spree. You decide where your comfort zone is.

Here is my modified version of the Abraham imaginary expand your wealth consciousness shopping spree by Esther and Jerry Hicks: I would encourage all of you to select the most expensive fabulous department store in your city (or neighboring city.) I want you to take a few minutes in your car to set your vibrational tone before you enter the store. I want you to thank the Universe for this beautiful luxurious elegant store, as it is evidence of great wealth and prosperity. I want you to bless the experience and the opportunity to surround yourself in such splendor.

Personally, I used to get knots in my stomach and feel bad about not having the money to shop in those stores. I would feel tears behind my eyes. Then one day, the thought hit me like a thunderbolt! I asked myself, "How can I attract wealth when I feel bad about being surrounded in it?"

So I decided to go to Neiman Marcus in Beverly Hills on my lunch breaks. At first I would have an imaginary $1,000 to spend. I entered the store and I would just breathe in the beauty. I would wander the store and touch and feel the luxury fabrics and closely examine how the most expensive items were made. I would hold the clothing up to me and imagine wearing each glorious garment. Then I would bless the experience and go back to work.

Eventually what you will find is that you can work up to spending $10,000 or more in this make-believe shopping tour. Why should you do this? You should do this in order to expand your wealth consciousness and let go of your limiting beliefs about money. I remember that soon I was having lunch at Neiman's, having a cocktail there after work, and feeling good about trying on the clothes. The knots in my stomach and the tears behind my eyes changed to joy, utter joy to be surrounded by such beauty. Within a few years, I was shopping at Neiman's and was one of their very good customers. I broke my own glass ceiling of limited wealth. You can do the same.

The irony of this is that once you feel good shopping in the most expensive stores, you start to open yourself up to getting all kinds of deals and discounts at fine stores. The salespeople call you first when items are getting marked down for sales. You become privy to the deepest discounts and shopping points that you may not have known about if you hadn't created a relationship with the sales associates. You can shop only at sale time if you choose and they will still value your business. Personally, I also like to shop for the regular priced items for the very special things I feel may never go on sale. But that's totally an individual choice.

You may wonder why I had to play the Abraham shopping game at all, given that I have spent my entire life in the fashion business. The truth is that about twelve years ago I lost almost all of my money and had to start over again. I had to dress very glamorously for work and had to do it on a dime. I could only shop at resale or deep discount stores. I knew if I wanted to change my life, I had to change how I thought and felt about money and luxury. I did exactly what I am telling you to do. Of course, I worked hard and did my affirmations. I meditated and prayed, but spending time in luxury stores and elegant restaurants made me feel that the world was my oyster once again.

Ironically because of this game, I became a super resale designer consignment shopper because I am not afraid to shop the best stores. I know when I see a deep discount on a designer piece of clothing, shoes or accessories. I know what the regular price is, so I know when it is marked down to a phenomenal price. I also know quality, because I have trained my eye to see it at a glance. You can do this too. Anyone can. You just have to be willing to push yourself out of your comfort zone. Now when I take my clients on resale shopping tours, I am able to tell them things like, "Oh my goodness, that designer suit was originally $2,500 and it's selling here for $500! You need to grab this one!"

To which they always reply, "How did you see that? How do you know?" I know because beauty is a vibration and when you understand and love beautiful things they come to you easily … as do all things you focus on with intention and love.

What is important to understand here, and what took me a long time to come to terms with myself, is that you are worthy of having those things that make you feel beautiful. You deserve to indulge in those garments and accessories that shout out your personality and essence, whether it be cashmere or silk or wonderful jeans, or a pair of earrings that sparkle like your eyes. The goal is to believe that you are entitled to be as glamorous, sexy, elegant, chic, and as fabulous as you can be. Toot your own horn, strut your stuff and exude your unique beauty in every wonderful detail of your wardrobe. Remember, you are worth it and you deserve it. Bless the energy it takes to be the most beautifully dressed person you can be. You will feel the rewards down to your soul each and every time you look in the mirror.

CHAPTER TEN

Head to Toe Beauty

"I walk in beauty." These words are part of an ancient Navajo poem.

Yes, I love to walk in beauty and what that means to me is walking in beautiful shoes: gorgeous high heels, fabulous boots, sexy sandals. All shapes, colors, fabrics, and leathers. Why? Because I can. Because I am a woman and because I know the power of beautiful shoes. Personally, I especially love high heels! Maybe if I were very tall I would like flats too, but I'm not, and I don't!

I applaud great shoes. I understand the effect they have on others and the way fabulous shoes make me feel. Most of all, I always remember that I get to wear beautiful shoes even when I don't have to. It is a choice and the attitude of my shoes determines my altitude! Literally!

The expression "put your best foot forward" should really be changed to "put your best shoes forward!" Men and women need to literally step it up in this country and fabulous shoes are the fastest way I know to do that.

Shoes have power. Tremendous power. A great pair of shoes can make old clothes look new. They can make us look modern, successful, and elegant. Shoes speak volumes about how we hold ourselves; in good esteem or not. Our entire attitude can be seen in our shoes. Shoes tell the world if we are simply practical or extravagantly stylish and every message in between. They point the way and begin every step. For men and for women, shoes can make or break our appearance. I just can't say enough about the value of great shoes!

In Europe, a person takes pride in his shoes. The average person may only have two or three pairs of shoes, but they are elegant. The best they can afford. Their shoes are stylish, polished and in good repair, and are comfortable to walk in. Europeans walk a lot. They are not sedentary people so they take care of their shoes. To Europeans, shoes are not an afterthought. They are an important part of their personal style.

Just the other day, a European friend of mine said she couldn't understand why Americans go around with unpolished, unkempt shoes. She said that in Europe people of any means don't wear their shoes like that; Europeans keep them polished and well heeled and in good repair. She isn't exaggerating about how bad the shoe situation is in America. My goodness, even President Obama's picture was taken during his election campaign with his feet up on his desk and large holes in the soles of his shoes. Some people may say that showed how hard he was campaigning. I would dare to say it showed how little attention he was paying to his shoes.

As an image consultant, I can't tell you how many times I have seen shoe horrors on executives and corporate professionals: shoes with holes in the soles; the leather uppers separating at the seams; scuffs and scrapes so deep the leather looked chewed up; women's heels all scraped off and the metal going clackity clack on someone's nice wood floors (dinging them terribly with every step!!) Apart from these offenses, I have seen nice outfits paired with old, out-of-style, worn-out shoes that made me cringe. I honestly can't understand what people are thinking! I guess they are not thinking … about their shoes that is.

Shoes are the most misunderstood of all accessories, especially in the U.S. If you ask most American women why they don't wear high heels, they'll say because they are not comfortable. Then why can women all over Europe wear high heels and walk on cobblestone streets (not to mention in Central and South America and many other countries)? They wear them because it's important to them and they understand that comfort and style are not enemies. High heels can be as comfortable for a woman as dress shoes can be for a man. It just takes knowledge and practice to find comfortable stylish shoes. In other words, it takes effort, which is something the majority of Americans seem unwilling to expend for their appearance.

A well-known author and new friend of mine told me that she "judges a book by its cover and people by their shoes!" When I asked her to explain, she expanded her belief by saying that she looks at a person's shoes to determine what they're about. Right on my sole sister!

I can't help but think back to a couple of years ago when my husband and I attended a jazz concert. I was wearing some fabulous sexy high heels and walking comfortably in them. My love of wearing them must have shown in every step. A well-to-do executive came and sat down next to me and said, "Great shoes! I think there is nothing sexier than a woman wearing high heels and being very comfortable in them." He continued by saying that he hates it when he sees women wearing heels looking like they are suffering, and even worse can't walk in them properly. "You mean they wobble around or stomp around in their heels?" I asked.

"Yes, and I cringe when I see women doing that, but you walk in those beautiful heels like they are an extension of your legs." To which I smiled and basked in the glow of my sexy shoes.

"Eve, are you going to teach us how to wear high heels comfortably? You promised us! We just don't understand how you stand there all day teaching in those heels! Aren't you in agony? We wish we could wear heels."

My students offer up every excuse on the planet as to why they can't buy heels, wear heels and enjoy heels. But almost every single student/client wants to, so I teach them the lost art of wearing heels and walking like a lady. It always delights me to see how hungry they are for this knowledge, even if they fight me at the beginning. I win them over and make them step into their power joyfully! You all have to understand that there are different shoes for different reasons. Some shoes are for walking. Some are for sitting and dining. Some are for dancing. And some are for wearing in bed!

You have to determine where you are wearing your shoes: work, play, or social occasions. Based on that and the strength of your legs will help you determine how high a heel you can wear. That's why it's so important to keep your legs, core and glutes strong ... so you can wear heels with greater ease. Of course, platforms on the soles of your shoes help make wearing high heels easier as they reduce the pitch of the shoe so the pressure is not as great on the balls of your feet.

The challenge is that most women don't realize that every woman's feet have a certain shape and pattern. The trick is to find a shoe designer whose shoe pattern matches the shape of your foot. It's crucial that the bend of the last (as the shape of the bottom of the shoe is referred to) match where the ball of your foot bends. In other words, for maximum comfort, the ball of your foot must line up perfectly at the right spot, so the bend of the shoe is under the ball of your feet, where most of the pressure of the shoes rests.

The weight of your body needs to be thrust back onto your heels, not the balls of your feet. This is crucial. If you feel like you are leaning forward in your shoes, then the balls of your feet will kill you and you won't be able to walk even one block comfortably! So pay careful attention to how your body aligns itself in those high heels.

You must also be able to wiggle your toes in your high heels. You never want your toes to feel pinched or cramped in your shoes. That is bad for the health of your feet and will most definitely be painful. If you are buying pointed-toed pumps, it helps to buy them a half size longer. This should compensate for the point and leave room for your toes if your feet swell from heat or being on your feet many hours at a time.

Never shop for shoes at the end of a long day on your feet as your feet may be swollen; unless you can return the shoes if they don't feel comfortable when you try them on at home. Always wear your shoes at home first to test them for comfort. Make sure you know the store's return policy, especially if you are buying a brand that you have never worn. You must see if their pattern works for your feet and you can't always tell that in the store until you get practice at buying heels in my method.

I think back to when I was only two years old. I still couldn't walk! I don't know why, but I can remember the doctor trying to put braces on my legs. I remember screaming and crying. I was so afraid. My father told me later he couldn't put me through that ordeal, so he asked the orthopedist to find another way to help me walk. The arches of my feet were so flat that I couldn't balance. The doctors decided to make me custom made boot shoes (that laced up above my ankles) and had metal arch supports inside of them. Those shoes were so ugly and I had to wear them until I was ten years old! But I learned to walk and run and dance. Every few months as I grew, my dad would take me to get fitted in a new pair of ugly medical looking shoes with uncomfortable arch supports.

My dad took pride in my appearance and although I only had one pair of shoes to wear to school, they were always clean and polished. I can still see him polishing my white orthopedic shoes lovingly. I think he got carried away because even the sides of the dark leather soles looked like they had white-out on them. But they were clean and that's what mattered to my dad. "Evaleh," he said (my nickname in Yiddish), "You must always take care of your shoes! You have to spend good money to buy the best shoes, the best food, and have the best dental care. Nothing else is as important!" I followed that advice as soon as I was old enough to buy my own shoes.

Oh, how I wanted to buy beautiful shoes! I dreamt of them. When I was a little girl, maybe nine years old, I would sneak on my French housekeeper's very high-heeled stilettos and walk around in them just to see what it was like to wear a womanly shoe. Of course, she would catch me every single time as she heard the clickety-clack of her pumps pounding loudly on the hardwood floors. She would scream at me in French and tell me that I would break her heels. She obviously coveted her high heels as much as I did! I would grudgingly take them off and give them back to her. Very grudgingly.

At the age of ten, I went for my final check-up to my orthopedic doctor. He said that I could now wear normal shoes! Then he told me something I would always remember. "Eve, your feet will do better if you wear heels. The higher heels will create an arch in your foot that you don't have. You should also walk on the sand and do ballet. This will strengthen the muscles of your feet and legs. Good luck and go get some pretty shoes!" And so my obsession with beautiful shoes began. It always amazed me that nowadays so many women in this country take their shoes for granted. In fact, I was thinking gorgeous shoes were almost a lost cause until Sarah Jessica Parker in Sex in the City loved her Manolos as much as I did! God bless her for making women fall in love with designer shoes. For me, though, the obsession goes deeper. For me, life is more beautiful when I walk in beautiful shoes. My energy changes and my vibration goes up along with my stature when I wear gorgeous stylish high-heels.

I think my passion for heels is contagious because every single student of mine always wants to learn more about buying, wearing, and walking in high heels. Once they learn, it's like a whole world of new shoe possibilities opens up to them. Everyone needs to know what this feels like. Everyone!

Be aware that many women buy the wrong size shoes. At a fine shoe store, they will have well-trained sales associates that know how to properly measure your feet. Weight loss or weight gain can affect your shoe size, as can pregnancy and menopause, water retention and the climate. It's good to re-check your shoe size periodically. And for heaven's sake, don't balk at buying a half to one size larger if the shoe runs small. No one is going to be looking inside your shoes for the size. Some brands run short and some run long. It's part of the process to learn how each shoe line fits you. That will make your future shoe shopping faster and more accurate.

Sometimes it's okay to have a pair of shoes stretched professionally at the shoe repair. If the shoes you are buying are made in a leather or suede that stretches a lot, then you would want to buy those shoes snug and have them stretched slightly before you wear them. Don't try to make your feet stretch the shoes, that can cause blisters and needless pain. But truthfully, when you try on new shoes, they really should (for the most part) fit and feel good. You should be able to walk in them steadily and comfortably. Nothing should feel forced. However, even the most comfortable new pair of shoes need to be broken in before you walk longer distances in them or wear them all day. It's best to break them in over two to three days; wearing them for more time each day. All fine leather shoes will mold themselves to your feet when you wear them. That's part of the process.

When trying on shoes, take your time to really feel the shoes. Notice if your vibration went up or down. Follow the same principles of clothes shopping by being aware of the color, texture, inner line, outer line, quality, construction, fit, fashion type, message it sends and where you will wear them. Price, once again, must be the last thing you consider. People seem to find the money for shoes that they love and they can get a lot of use from. Buy less pairs and buy smart. Buy great shoes at discounters or resale consignment stores if the regular retail price is too high. Again, the mindset needs to be on quality, not quantity if money and the space to store them are an issue.

I am always amazed at how many homeless people in Beverly Hills comment on my shoes! They are hungry and asking for help to passersby. Yet, their faces light up when they see my shoes! Oh, the comments I get from them like, "Oh girl, I love your shoes!" or "My goodness those are fabulous boots!" It's almost like it makes them happy to see beautiful shoes. You may not believe me, but I swear it's true. Male or female, rich or poor; everyone loves to see beautiful shoes.

Men need to follow the same shopping formula and advice when buying shoes. They need to consider the shopping order of importance and follow the concepts. The only difference is the way men get their shoes fitted. For men, comfort is of primary importance. They innately know when their shoes fit properly; therefore, men need to focus more on style and different shoes for different work and lifestyle needs. Most men don't put enough thought into their shoes or their socks, for that matter. Shoes are extremely important for a man because as a rule, men wear far fewer accessories than women. So a man's shoes can speak volumes about who he is and where he is going.

It's mandatory that everyone has a fantastic shoe repair person at their disposal! This is essential for maintaining your shoes and modifying them occasionally. The shoe repair can make your shoes more water resistant, lower the heels slightly, add special padding under the lining, re-dye the color, and remove stains. A good shoe repair specialist can even take in your tall boots to fit your slim calves, add a slight platform under the sole for comfort, and an ankle strap to keep the shoes from slipping off your slim feet. Knowing your options is key to making the most of your shoes. The shoe repair shop can also fix your handbags and other leather goods.

Cedar shoe trees are a must for men's shoes. They help keep the original shape of the shoes intact. They draw out the excess moisture from the leather. An average person loses about sixteen ounces per day of moisture from their feet and into their shoes. The cedar draws out the moisture and allows the shoe to retain its original shape. Women can use cedar shoe trees too, but most don't. It's often difficult to fit them into the huge variance of styles and shapes of women's shoes. However, shoe trees are great for women's boots and really helps keep them looking new.

It's also crucial for everyone to rotate the shoes they wear and never wear the same pair every day unless you absolutely have to. As I said, the feet release a lot of moisture into our shoes; therefore, by giving your shoes a chance to rest for twenty-four to forty-eight hours, you give moisture and odors a chance to leave. This will extend the life of your shoes and make wearing them far more pleasant. This will also make being close to you more pleasant, if you get my drift!

In order for your new shoes to be a home run, you have to know how to walk in your shoes. Women need to lift their feet up nicely by leading with their knees in the direction they want to go and letting their feet follow. This will give them a more feminine polished walk. Women also need to add a slight subtle sway to their hips so they don't look like men clomping around in their fancy shoes.

I put on the song, "I'm Too Sexy!" for my bootcamp and I make all the women line up and take turns, one at a time, walking as femininely as they can across the room. They pretend that the most handsome man they have ever seen is interested. He stares from across the room. Now they prance around in their high heels for their pretend admirer.

Over and over we play that song and my students try to walk like models doing the catwalk. Most of them, sadly, are so out of their feminine essence that they have trouble learning how to walk like a woman. They are disconnected from their hips so instead of gliding across the room, they stomp, they clomp and they hippity hop, all of which makes me realize how desperately we need finishing schools again in this country! We have tried too hard to break the glass ceiling of female job discrimination for so many decades that in the process we have forgotten how to move like women.

"Eve! I just don't get how to walk like this!" I hear repeatedly.

"Marissa, show this woman how to walk," I say to my assistant. *"You walk and have her walk behind you holding on to your hips so she can feel the motion of your hips. It takes work and awareness to walk like a woman. It takes desire and practice too. It's worth the effort, believe me. You will feel differently down to your core. It will awaken your feminine being. Your essence will shift in a most positive way. A woman can be dressed beautifully with perfect hair and makeup, but if she walks like a horse or clomps around town like a man, she will never look her best. More than perfection, men are drawn to women who love being a woman … who are comfortable in their skin. It's called being authentic and along with that comes confidence. A woman who knows how to walk displays a lovely inner strength that is indescribable."*

A few years ago, my husband and I were taking ballroom dancing lessons in Beverly Hills, California. Our instructor was a phenomenal dancer who also happened to be gay. I loved dancing with him because he taught me so many things about staying in my feminine zone. One day while we were dancing, he stopped abruptly and said, "Eve, pull your ankles together between steps! Your legs are so wide apart that it looks like the Holland Tunnel! I could drive a car between them!"

"What?" I asked, mortified! "What do you mean?"

To which David replied, "I mean you need to dance like a woman. Stand like a woman and move like a woman."

David then demonstrated how I should bring my feet together. I said, "Wow, what makes you think you know so much about how a woman should move?"

Then he stopped, looked me in the eyes and said, "I'm twice the man you'll ever have and three times the woman you'll ever be!" I laughed until I cried and I have walked like a woman ever since: legs closed, lesson learned!

HOSIERY & SOCKS

You've got the shoes and you are walking the walk. Now you need to turn your attention to your socks if you're a man, and hosiery if you're a woman. If women go with nude legs, then their legs must be smooth and the color even. Women who opt for nude legs can wear leg makeup for a more finished look. Ladies, when you wear stockings be aware that they don't have snags, runs and holes.

Men's socks need to match either their slacks or their outfit. They can be solid or patterned. FYI, women notice a man's socks and we love when they are patterned and fashionable. Yes, women love looking at great socks, but don't like looking at your hairy legs poking out of your slacks because your socks are too short! So please do the "cross your legs" test to see if your socks are tall enough. Check to see that the elastic of your socks is in good condition and there are no holes in your heels or toes! That is such a turn-off and sends a signal of poverty, not success.

Aside from shoes and hosiery, I can't say enough about the importance of using the finest leather goods you can afford: wallet, handbag, briefcase, portfolio case and belts. All your leather goods must be polished and in good repair.

Always keep in mind, that since the advent of relaxed casual dress and business casual, it's a man's watch, belt, shoes and leather goods that speak of his status and success. For a woman it's her hair, makeup, hands, shoes, and handbags that determine how classy she looks.

CHAPTER ELEVEN

Great Grooming and Understanding Underwear

As a society, we need to talk about the G word. It's okay. I am referring to "grooming" and it needs to be good! There is simply no faster way to look on top of your game than by great grooming. As a rule, demented people don't usually groom themselves. Depressed people are often a mess. Successful, intelligent, positive people groom well or at least that's the perception. And always remember that how you are perceived is how you will be received.

As an image consultant, I have been hired by numerous companies to teach their executives how to groom properly! I am not kidding. One time I was hired to help a middle-management executive learn how to floss and brush her teeth, among other grooming problems! Can you imagine that I had to tell an educated woman that she needed to take better care of her dental hygiene because it was so offensive to her co-workers? I have had to tell corporate employees to iron their clothing, get new shoes (to replace worn-out disgusting smelly shoes), to use deodorant, to clean off their dandruff, to shave the wool out of their ears, and worse! Mind you, these were gainfully employed intelligent men and women yet they didn't know how to groom themselves properly and this was hurting their chance for promotion or continued employment. What a tragedy!

Once when I was at a business networking party, a well-to-do man in his late forties actually said to me, "Eve, you are an image consultant, right? What do you think I need?"

"Do you honestly want to know right here and now?" I asked.

"Yes," he said.

"Okay, you need to clean out that ball of wool sticking out of your ears!"

Yes, I have had to tell men to "eighty-six" the unibrow; I have had to brush men's eyebrows straight up their foreheads so they could see how horribly long they were; I have had to ask men to saw their toenails down because they were so disgustingly long and they had the nerve to wear flip-flops and let the world see them!

When I was a personal shopper, I had female clients in my dressing room whose bras were so dirty I refused to shop for them unless they bought a new clean bra. I have had to tell clients' employees to freshen their breath, wash their hair, clean their fingernails, and more. I have seen job hunters not get hired because they showed up in a dirty car. Yes, the bosses look at everything. I mean everything! I have seen employees not get promoted because they didn't look successful enough. I have had girlfriends tell me they couldn't date a guy who otherwise seemed very nice because his grooming was so offensive. After many years as an image consultant, I have seen it all and it never fails to amaze me how terrible people's grooming habits can be.

In regard to grooming, it helps to think of yourself as a beautiful kitchen. Imagine how good this kitchen looks when it's all clean, scrubbed and polished: windows clean and sparkling, stainless steel buffed, and the entire room smelling fragrant, curtains washed, shutters dusted and everything neatly in its place. There's nothing quite as refreshing.

Now imagine this same kitchen with a dirty filthy stove, food splattered all over it. The oven is greasy. Dirty dishes are pilled up in the sink. The floors are full of scuff marks and crumbs. The garbage pail is full and overflowing with leftovers and other unpleasant odors. The white porcelain sink is stained and yellowed. Dust is thick and clinging onto the lighting fixture and cabinet tops. Not only is this not very inviting, it is rather repulsive, wouldn't you agree?

When we are well groomed, we feel and look much better. Does it take consistent effort? Yes, and it also takes time and money. Just like having a great image, great grooming requires all three. The rewards are instant and tangible. People will be drawn to you. They will respect you more and think you are better at whatever you do. You will look refreshed and rejuvenated. People will think you are more on your A-game. Watch and notice the changes as you step up your grooming habits.

I have listed my top grooming tips. I hope you will all follow this advice and take it seriously. It is the fastest least expensive way to look more polished and successful. You can never be too well groomed for yourself or for business. Trust me, never!

EVE'S TOP 20 GROOMING TIPS FOR WOMEN AND MEN:

- **Bathing:** Shower or bathe at least once a day. Twice a day if necessary due to weather and activity level. Use a loofah or body scrubbing exfoliating gloves to remove dead dry skin all over your body, making your skin smooth to the touch.

- **Hair:** Your hair must always be clean, smell nice and be well-styled. If you have dandruff or other scalp conditions, take care of it so no one notices flakes on your clothing. Cut your hair on a regular basis so that it falls into place easily and looks well-kempt.

- **Hair color:** As a general rule, color as often as needed to keep your color fresh and the roots from showing. You can touch up your grey roots at home with hair mascara or root re-growth tint or special colored powders. Nothing looks worse than grey roots on the top of your head and around your face. People see it even if they don't say anything. The rule with hair color is this: if you are going to color your hair, then maintain it properly!

- **Fingernails and toenails:** You will need to have a weekly manicure for natural nails, every other week for acrylic, gels or shellac nails. Remove unsightly hangnails and cuticles. Keep your fingernails clean, well-trimmed and shaped at all times! No exceptions! Pedicures are a must every 2–3 weeks, no matter who else sees them!

- **Feet:** I suggest that you use a pumice stone, nail file or callous remover in between pedicures so that your feet are smooth and soft. Avoid having ugly, cracked dry skin on your heels, bottom of your feet and toes. If you have athlete's foot, take care of it. Nothing is more unsightly and unsexy than unkempt feet!

- **Teeth:** Always floss your teeth at least once a day. Brush them 2–3 times a day. Check your teeth after each meal to be certain they are clean. Check your breath frequently. Carry a breath freshener with you. Have good dental care.

Get your teeth cleaned at least twice a year. Whiten your teeth if they need it. Have cracks and gaps filled. A white beautiful smile makes you look more educated, successful and sexy. You are worth the investment!

- **Deodorant**: Use deodorants and anti-perspirant daily. It is healthier to use a natural deodorant that doesn't block your lymph glands. Always be aware of any body odors.

- **Lotion**: This is a must for everyone! Moisturize your body after bathing or showering. Keep your hands soft and smooth.

- **Body Hair**: Women should be hair-free all over their bodies: face, armpits, arms, and legs. Men need to get rid of any nasal and ear hair that shows. Yes, everyone can see it and it looks terrible! Genital hair should be minimal to none depending on your personal preference. All pubic hair must be groomed. Wild bushes are not okay, for anyone!

- **Perfume**: Apply perfumes and cologne sparingly for work. Your perfume or cologne should never enter a room before you do or linger after you leave. People should only smell it when they get very close to you. Many people are allergic to scents. For your personal or social time, you can wear more perfume according to who you are with and what they like.

"Eve! What is that delicious scent? You smell like a cookie!" people always comment.

"*Oh, that's my vanilla perfume. I always layer it with my other fragrances.*" I reply. "*Because a girl always has to smell good enough to eat!!*

"*I am sure you have all heard the old saying, 'Always wear clean underwear in case you get into a car accident?' I prefer to think about it this way, 'Always wear fabulous underwear in case you get lucky!' We never know when the opportunity arises.*"

Every woman in my boot camp roars with laughter as I smile my mischievous smile with a sparkle in my eyes!

- **Pre and Post Coital Cleansing**: Be very clean all over, and I mean all over before having sex. Make sure you wash up well after, too, for your own sake and your partner's!

- **Eyebrows**: Both men and women need to groom their eyebrows. Unibrows are not attractive, neither are bushy long eyebrow hairs. Very distracting! Women should have their eyebrows professionally arched: tweezed, threaded or waxed. Men should have theirs waxed and trimmed as part of their grooming maintenance routine.

- **Clothing**: Must be clean, pressed, lint-free and in good repair. No loose buttons, broken zippers or ripped seams please! Your clothing must fit properly at all times. If it's too small or too loose, don't wear it. People will notice.

- **Shoes:** All of your shoes must be polished and clean. The heels must be in good condition and never worn down. Check your soles and have them repaired as necessary. Don't skimp! Take your shoes to a shoe repair regularly for polishing and maintenance. Use shoe trees as needed.

- **Handbags, Briefcases and Portfolio Cases**: Never ever over-stuff your leather cases. Keep them organized, clean inside and out, and well-maintained. Make certain they always coordinate with your outfit and are in good repair. Never treat your handbag or business case like a garbage bag! Clean it out regularly.

- **Hair and Makeup Brushes**: Wash and clean these regularly.

- **Jewelry**: Even your jewelry needs to be clean and shiny. Keep your gemstones clean and your silver pieces polished. They are meant to be worn clean, not gunked up and dirty.

- **Hosiery and Socks**: Holes, snags, and runs are not acceptable for your hosiery or socks … at any time! The elastic must be in good repair and never worn-out. Belts: Need to be the right size and in good condition. The belt holes may not be worn-out and the leather must be in fine condition. Yes, your belts get old and worn-out and need to be updated like your other leather goods.

- **Your Car:** Your car is an investment and speaks volumes about you when it isn't clean and well-maintained. Never leave garbage strewn around in your car. Wash it regularly and get it detailed at least 1–2 times a year. Everything looks better when it's clean and polished, including your vehicle.

- **Lingerie & Underwear:** Your underwear is never supposed to show at work. Be aware of stray bra straps, slips peeking out or underwear lines showing through. Check your outfit from all angles with a mirror to see if your undergarments are visible and if you have any unsightly bulges coming through your clothes.

I would be remiss if I didn't mention my thoughts about tattoos because tattoos have become so widely used and accepted by people from all walks of life. However, since they are for the most part permanent, unless you go to great lengths to have them removed, you need to really think about what type of tattoo you get and where you place it. Tattoos can be discreet like underwear or an extremely powerful and visible part of a person's image. So like the rest of your image, I suggest you give a lot of thought to what type of tattoos you decide on getting and match them with the image you want to project. Keep in mind those tattoos may speak volumes about your image no matter what you wear if they're visible ... so think carefully about what those tattoos will express about you and your professional goals before the ink touches your skin.

Back to grooming. Men, it's not cute to see a white t-shirt peeking through the collar of your dress shirt. Your underpants need to be clean, fit you well, flatter your physique as well as be comfortable. Hopefully someone gets to see you in them, and even if they don't, you deserve to have nice underpants. Women hate to look at worn-out ill fitting "tidy whities." Nothing is more offensive than stained and/or yellowed white underwear and t-shirts. Having nice fitting underwear is part of good grooming and dressing well. If they are not stain-free and have holes in them, replace them immediately!

Men also have the option nowadays to buy slimming undershirts that help conceal midriff bulges and slim the abdominal area. You also have many options for styles of undershirts, underpants, and socks. Take time to shop for the best quality you can afford. Then keep it all clean and in good repair. Wear the right undershirt and underpants for your clothing. For example, black underpants look terrible under white pants! Black socks don't belong with white shoes. Last but not least, dress socks don't belong on your feet with shorts!

Ladies, you need to have a lingerie arsenal in your closet! With all the different styles, fabrics, necklines, and cuts of clothing styles we wear, not one style of bra and panties will suffice. Know your options and what you need for your particular body shape and weight. Get the right bra, panties, camisoles, slips, half-slips and smoothing garments (if necessary). Use a mirror to see if your lingerie is creating unnecessary bumps and bulges. Panty lines may be a turn on to some, but they're not pretty or appropriate at work. Neither is see-through clothing.

No one wants to see a woman's cellulite through her pants. And your bra showing isn't okay for work unless you are in certain lines of work such as the pleasure industry or the entertainment field. I suggest every woman get professionally fitted in her bra to make certain her bust line looks its best. Most women are wearing the wrong bra size and the wrong type of bra. There are so many shapes and styles of bras and panties. Study up on your lingerie options.

Wash your bras every one to two wearings and panties after every use. Think of your bra like a white t-shirt. You could never wear that more than once or twice. Bras are the same. The straps and backs get dirty quickly. Hand wash your lingerie or machine wash in a lingerie bag with special delicate detergent that won't damage the elastic, and then drip dry. If you gain or lose weight, have your lingerie altered accordingly or buy new ones to fit you. Nothing will make you feel more like a woman than having gorgeous, clean, perfectly fitted bras, panties and undergarments. You deserve to have whatever touches your skin first to be as sensational as you are.

"How many of you ladies know to wash your bras every one to two wearings?" I ask my boot camp attendees. Out of eighteen to twenty women, only one to two usually raise their hands each time. You can't believe it, right? I can't either. No one is teaching us the basics of grooming anymore and it's sad. Feeling good all over and under is the key to good grooming. It really is a matter of self-respect and respect for others. It is smart to be well-groomed and it's considerate. Being dirty is like serving someone a good glass of wine in a dusty stained goblet. It ruins the experience.

All kidding aside, you will never be sorry that you are well-groomed.

CHAPTER TWELVE

Personal Dress Code Commitment

The powerful concept of having Dress Codes in this country can only be effective when combined with the implementation of Personal Dress Codes. We must have the courage and tenacity to ask ourselves in every situation: What can I do to represent myself, my family, my job, my company and my country in the best possible way? By doing this, we begin to realize that looking our best is not about us as individuals, but rather about us as a nation. This is the mindset that we so desperately need: teamwork and pride.

We have an important choice to make as we are now at a crossroads in America. We can choose to continue to look like a nation of slobs asleep at the wheel or like a nation of amazingly modern innovators, leaders and inventors. I choose amazing! I want that for me and I want that for our country. I believe in order for us to survive, as the leader of the free world, there is no other choice. There is no room for mediocrity, only excellence and that excellence must begin with every American. We are the America the world sees. We are the America that travels abroad. We are "the people" and we can make a huge positive difference if we want to. This is an enormous responsibility that we can no longer afford to take lightly.

We have let the pendulum swing from the strict rigid fashion rules of the 50s and 60s to where we are now: fashion anarchy with no rules and no boundaries. We have to make quality important again and we desperately need to display quality in all that we do: our education, our products, our health and in our image (personally and collectively as a nation). Of course, there is a percentage of Americans who dress well and care about their image, but the percentage is way too small. We need to turn that percentage around and fast! We can do it. Americans have always harnessed a powerful force for change when we feel threatened. Well, our way of life IS being threatened and it's more from our own complacency than from outside forces. We have allowed this mess to happen and we alone can change the situation.

I am always sad as my boot camps come to a close. I gather everyone around me to share my final thoughts. All the participants are glowing and excited to go home and share their makeovers and all they have learned. The air is electric.

"You have all learned valuable image information and skills during the three days we have spent together in my Beauty Boot Camp. I have shared with you the basics of creating a great image. You have all learned what makes you special and unique. You have participated in your own makeovers and you all look fabulous! I am so proud of the progress you have made and the courage you had to be here. You have taken a stand for beauty and I know now that the light bulb has been turned on in your heads about the power of image, you will never look at image the same way again. You have been awakened to a new way of looking and being. You have learned a vast amount of knowledge and information in these three long days. Most of this knowledge can be put into immediate practice and I encourage you all to do that. Pay attention to the way your energy shifts as you continue to improve your image and re-enter the real world, your world. Pay attention to how much better you get treated. Pay attention to how the doors open easier and pay attention to how you feel. You must experience this for yourselves. There is no way I can describe the many ways your lives will improve as you treat your image with the respect it deserves."

Each and every person who is reading this book, taking my Image and Beauty Boot Camps, or working with me privately has a desire to improve his or her image and increase their success in life. The difference between you and the person who has a great image is not the amount of money you have. You don't have to be rich to be well dressed as I said earlier. No, it is the desire to improve and the tenacity to follow through with new disciplines. It is about seeing the value of an effective personal appearance.

The main difference between a person who looks great and one who doesn't comes down to attitude and habits. The well-dressed, well-groomed person says, "Of course, why not?" While the disheveled person moans and groans, "Why? This is so much work! Do I have to?" You can easily see by now that it's your attitude that determines your altitude in life, individually and more importantly as a nation.

Habits take time to change and to create. Be tenacious and consistent. You are worth it. When you feel lazy and don't want to follow through, think of the example you are setting for your children, your spouse or partner, your co-workers, etc.

You have stepped into the light and there is no turning back. You are all my ambassadors of elegance, beauty and style. You matter. Your manners matter and so does the way you behave. The world needs you and so does our country. You will be like a beacon of light. The positive effect you will have on others will radiate out in ways you can never imagine.

I encourage you to do whatever it takes to keep being your best and enjoy this journey of self-love and self-respect. Remember as I said earlier, having a good image takes time, money and effort and it takes consistent work. After a few months, you will form good habits that will serve you well the rest of your life.

As we increase our desire to be world-class leaders once again, we have no more time for laziness and excuses. The Chinese, the Indians, the Brazilians and other industrious nations are surpassing us with their work ethic, education and desire to excel.

Our individual complacency has infected us as a nation and now we must work hard to heal and maintain our previous status as the leading nation in the world. We must ask ourselves every day if we are representing this nation with excellence. This search begins with how we care for ourselves: our image, our grooming, our manners and our health. We cannot look to our government to do what we are unwilling to do for our families and ourselves. We are not victims! We live in a nation where anyone can achieve his or her dreams and live in excellence. We must never ever take that for granted.

You are now a privileged student of my Fast Track to Fabulous™ program. And as such you *get to* make the following commitments to yourself. Remember that it takes thirty days to create a habit and ninety days to make it yours for a lifetime. I strongly suggest that you faithfully follow through on these commitments for thirty days, then another thirty, and then thirty more. After ninety days, you will be on your way to a lifetime of beauty, enhanced self-respect and class.

Please fill in your name neatly in the blank space below. Putting your name to these commitments reinforces your desire to improve yourself now! You are making a commitment for the next ninety days to do the following with an attitude of gratitude.

I, _____ faithfully commit to do the following for a minimum of ninety days:

Image Commitments for Women:
I will take my image seriously and strategize my image.
I will dress well 24/7 wherever I go.
I will allow myself 30–60 minutes every morning to prepare myself to face the world.
I will wear makeup every day even if I stay at home.
I will reapply my lipstick during the day and powder my nose (and/or remove shine from oily areas of my face).
I will dress in my best colors and be well coordinated.
I will make certain that my clothing is clean, well-pressed, in good repair and fits me perfectly.
I will wear the sexiest, most stylish shoes I can.
I will wear bras and panties that match, fit me properly, make me feel sexy and flatter my body in my clothing.
I will use the best handbag I can afford and keep it neat and not over stuff it.
I will wear the right accessories to coordinate with my outfit.
I will keep my wardrobe updated, modern and stylish.
I will focus on quality, not quantity for my clothing, shoes, handbags and accessories.
I will keep my car clean inside and out, as it is part of my image.

Image Commitments for Men:
I will never leave the house unless I am immaculately groomed, styled, and well-dressed and coordinated, 24/7.
I will take my image seriously and strategize my image every day.
I will dress in a way that is consistent with who I am and what I want to become.

I will wear clothing in my most flattering colors.

I will make certain that my clothing is clean, well-pressed, tailored to my body, fits me properly and is in good repair.

I will wear nice underwear that is new looking, fits me well and is flattering to my physique.

I will wear the best leather goods I can afford.

I will opt for quality, not quantity in everything I wear.

I will update my wardrobe seasonally to keep it modern and stylish.

I will wear fashionable shoes that coordinate with my clothing.

I will wear the finest watch I can afford.

I will keep my briefcase neat and well organized.

Grooming Commitments for Women:

I will never, ever sleep with makeup on.

I will shower or bathe at least once a day or more, as needed.

I will scrub my body at least 2–5 times a week, so my skin is soft to the touch.

I will shave, wax and trim my body hair on a consistent basis.

I will use nice bath gels and lotions on my body.

I will strive to keep my complexion clean, exfoliated, smooth and hydrated.

I will make sure that my fingernails and toenails are manicured at all times, even in the winter, with no chips in the polish.

I will style my hair daily, even on the days I don't wash it.

I will keep my eyebrows groomed and body hair waxed or shaved.

I will wash my bra after 1–2 wearings.

I will only wear shoes that are polished and in good repair.

I will have my clothing altered as needed.

I will not wear stockings that have snags, holes or runs in them.

I will floss daily and brush my teeth at least twice a day.

I will carry breath freshener and check my teeth after meals.

If I wear perfume, I will be certain it is lightly applied.

I will keep my closet clean, dust-free and coordinated.

Grooming Commitments for Men:
I will shower at least once a day or more as needed.
I will floss daily and brush my teeth at least twice a day.
I will comb my hair during the day, as needed, remove oils off my face, and check that my teeth are clean after meals.
I will get my eyebrows professionally waxed and keep my body hair trimmed, waxed, and/or shaved as needed.
I will never ever go to bed without washing up.
I will keep my complexion clean, clear, smooth and free of blackheads.
I will get a facial periodically as needed.
I will wear deodorant and smell fresh.
If I wear cologne, I will wear it lightly.
I will make certain my fingernails and toenails are clean and well-manicured at all times.
I will style my hair daily, even when I don't wash it.
I will trim/remove my stray nasal hairs and ear hairs (inside and out).
I will keep my shoes polished and in good repair, odor free.
I will never wear ugly underwear or torn pajamas to bed.
I will keep my closet clean, dust-free and well coordinated.

Attitude Commitments for Women:
I will say my positive affirmations 3 times a day *and believe them*.
I will hold myself in high esteem.
I will not say negative things about myself or to myself.
I will remember that I am a "Goddess" and I am "worth it."
I will expect the best for my life.
I will treat myself like a first-class woman.
I will appreciate myself, my life and the people in my life.
I will laugh more, love more, and enjoy more.
I will stay in my feminine power and allow men to be in theirs.
I will remember that beauty comes in all shapes and sizes.

Attitude Commitments for Men:
I will say my positive affirmations daily and *believe them*.
I will hold myself in high esteem.

I will not say negative things about myself or to myself.
I will remember that I am a "first-class" man and act accordingly.
I will expect the best for myself and my life.
I will be a gentleman at all times: polite and respectful.
I will pick-up after myself, be considerate, and let my loved ones know how much I appreciate them.
I will treat women with the utmost respect.
I will appreciate myself, my life and the people in my life.
I will laugh more, love more and enjoy more.

Health Commitments for Men and Women:
I will eat 3 healthy meals and 2–3 healthy snacks per day.
I will eat smaller portions of food and opt for quality over quantity.
I will read labels and be aware of eating natural, fresh, wholesome foods.
I will avoid processed foods, chemicals and preservatives.
I will drink plenty of water (with lemon).
I will get 7–8 hours of sleep per night.
I will meditate and/or pray daily to center myself.
I will take time to nourish, nurture and pamper myself daily if only for 15–30 minutes.
I will exercise 3–5 times a week: cardio, weight resistance and stretching.
I will take the supplements and vitamins my body needs.
I will respect my body and do what it takes to have excellent health, vitality, and energy.
I will affirm my body is regenerating and rejuvenating.

I have made these commitments in order to honor my life and myself. Only joy and goodness can come from actualizing these habits and putting them into daily practice.

Now you are all my ambassadors of beauty. Take that seriously and do me proud. Better yet, do yourselves proud.

EPILOGUE

Instituting Modern Dress Codes and Guidelines

We need to stand up for what is right in this country. We need to let go of fear and create positive changes that help us look our best and be our best. As all good parents know, we sometimes have to do things that aren't popular for the best interest of our children. Sometimes our children will kick and scream about a rule we enforce, but they will love us later, because we did it for their own good. In the same spirit, we can't be afraid to bring back dress codes and guidelines, because we are worried about upsetting people. People who dress well will be thrilled. The people who don't will be furious that their rights are being trampled. They haven't cared for years about how they have trampled the rights of those of us who *do care* about our appearance. So let's do what's in the best interest of our national success and make the relevant modifications to our standard of dress. We will all benefit in the long run.

We have tried total fashion anarchy and it isn't working. Our productivity is down, our economy isn't thriving as it could and the majority of people are depressed. As I see it, we don't have anything to lose by dressing better. Things can only go up from here because the pendulum can't go any further. I don't know about you, but I am tired of worrying if the person sitting on the airplane next to me has bothered to bathe that day. I don't want to see any more butt cracks staring up at me when people bend over. I certainly don't want to look at any more grungy, dirty, unkempt toenails in worn-out flip-flops. It's enough! It's not pretty and it's definitely not sexy!

It is important that you recognize that I am not advocating the dress codes of fifty years ago, that would be ridiculous in today's society. I do not think all men need to wear suits and ties to work. Nor am I saying that I want women dressed in bullet bras, girdles and dresses only. While I admit that would be fun for a moment, it is too dated.

What I am saying is that we need guidelines and rules that create positive boundaries. It's for our own good. There is nothing wrong, as I see it, with businesses demanding respectful dress for their establishments. They shouldn't need to be afraid that they may lose business if they ask people to dress to a certain standard. Corporations should be able to create dress guidelines and expectations for their employees. It's important for productivity and for enhanced professionalism. Dress codes will actually make it easier and less confusing for their employees to dress properly for work.

Dress codes take much of the confusion out of knowing what's expected and appropriate, which can be cost effective for two reasons. One, people won't waste money on the wrong clothing for work. Two, dressing properly can greatly enhance one's chances for success.

For over fifteen years, I have heard management complain about employee dress abuses and I've wondered for years why we are reluctant to speak out in favor of dress codes. Why is it that people who take the time to dress well have to keep silent while people who don't care how they look offend us and lower our morale? As I've said many times, you can do one of two things with your image when people look at you. You can either make them happier or depress them. Either way, your image will have an effect.

Dress codes are a good thing, as long as they are instituted fairly and across the board. Companies and their human resource departments can create them specifically for each department within the organization. Sales associates, for example, need to dress differently than the IT department. But that doesn't mean that the IT team can show up to work looking like they rolled out of bed! On the contrary, they still need to dress respectfully for work.

I suggest that businesses wanting to create dress guidelines do so by printing easy to follow dress codes and having every employee review them and sign them on the same day. It's also helpful to have a visual demonstration by a local department store as to what is considered appropriate dress. It would be fair to give employees thirty to sixty days notice so they have time to prepare any wardrobe modifications. There must also be written consequences for failure to adhere to the dress codes and these too must be printed up and handed out at the same time as the dress codes. This way the employees know what the new expectations are and the specific consequences for non-compliance. It must be fair and clear.

It's important in this economy that people realize they don't have to buy new wardrobes to be dressed properly at work. All that's usually needed is one to two nice blouses or shirt, a good fitting basic pair of slacks or skirt, and a decent pair of shoes. Maybe you will need one or two suits. Start with what you can afford. Keep it clean and in good repair. Then build your wardrobe over time focusing on the basics you have learned in this book. Remember, its quality, not quantity in your clothing that will give you the greatest value and best appearance.

During the Great Depression, many people only had one or two outfits to wear, but they managed to look decent and presentable. Where there is a will, there is a way. If we want something badly enough, we will find a way to make it happen.

I would also encourage any retail establishments to post upcoming dress codes and the date they will start being enforced in easily visible areas. For example, restaurants could put placards on their tables that say, "Starting on Jan 1, 2013, no patron will be allowed to wear shorts or flip-flops to our restaurant. We appreciate your cooperation." Flip-flops were never allowed in restaurants until recently. They are not sanitary and I am convinced they are a huge reason for the demise of dressing well.

In my opinion, if enough establishments and businesses create dress guidelines at the same time, the general public will have to improve their appearance. That doesn't mean that we can't dress casually to a casual or fast-food restaurant; we can still look clean, neat, and well-groomed. It is our social responsibility to do so.

Think about this: many restaurants and bars in this country spend a fortune to create a beautiful ambiance and décor for their patrons. Why is it acceptable for the patrons to disrespect the establishment by showing up disheveled, unclean and inappropriately dressed? Where is the fairness in that?

Recently, some restaurants have started an "adults only" rule: no children under the age of twelve allowed. At first, they were afraid that people would boycott them. But their business actually increased as their patrons were thrilled with this rule. I would venture to say that many people will also applaud dress code standards.

What about when people pay over $100 for a theatre ticket only to find the masses walking in looking like they are ready to go grocery shopping? What's fair about that? I know my family and friends want to be surrounded with people who also care about their appearance when they go to a special event. Who says the rights of the slovenly trump the rights of the well-dressed? Since when did our society become so flippant about spending over $100 to go to a concert or the theatre and think that it's not special? It IS special and we NEED to dress accordingly, in a special way that shows respect for what we are doing.

It's almost as if we have become *voyeurs* of glamour in this country. We want to *watch* how celebrities and the rich and famous dress. We are thrilled by their glamour, but don't care enough about how we look. The other day, I was on the airport rental car shuttle at LAX. There was a young family: a dad, a mom and their baby. The dad was wearing furry house slippers instead of shoes! I thought, "If the dad wears slippers in public, what will his son wear in fifteen years?" To add insult to injury, I saw a young man board the plane in flannel pajama bottoms. This fashion anarchy has to stop! It is madness. Embarrassing madness!

Money is not a reason to be badly dressed. People use that as an excuse. I don't believe that someone becomes well-dressed and groomed once they have money if they never cared about their looks in the first place. It's the same with being generous. People don't magically become generous and give to charities once they have money. People who are truly generous give even when they have a small amount to offer.

It is the intention behind everything we do that matters. Having a good appearance is a matter of one's intention, clear and simple.

I love this country. I am grateful to live here. I want to see us be the best we can be. I have devoted my life to helping people look and feel more beautiful. On that note, isn't one of our most beloved national songs entitled "America the Beautiful?"

According to Dr. Daniel Hammermesh, professor of economics and author of the book *Beauty Pays* (who I interviewed on my radio show) "Beautiful people earn about $274,000 more in their lifetime than ugly people." In his esteemed opinion after years of research, beauty pays!

Major League Baseball recently created a dress code for their Media Rooms. All media/journalists covering any MLB baseball game in this country must now dress to a certain professional standard.

Who is willing to step up to the bat next and help me make America beauty-full? It's got to be YOU!

JACQUIEJORDANINCPUBLISHING.COM • TVGUESTPERT.COM

ALSO PUBLISHED BY JACQUIE JORDAN INC.

Alex Detail's Revolution
by Darren Campo

Alex Detail has been kidnapped.

Again.

Ten years ago, Alex was a child genius who saved the world from The Harvesters, a mysterious alien force that attempted to extinguish Earth's sun.

A decade later, The Harvesters have returned, but Alex is no longer a prodigy and unwilling to fight another war. So someone at The House of Nations had him drugged and placed on the last remaining ARRAY warship, which is under heavy attack. Unfortunately for Alex's mysterious kidnappers (and the world) he has lost the mega IQ that allowed him to win the last war.

Now Alex must convince the ship's food-obsessed Captain Odessa to use his risky command program to save their ship, uncover his kidnapper's devious plot, and survive the war long enough to make it to Pluto, where, underneath the planet's frozen surface lies the only force in the universe that can stop The Harvesters.

JACQUIEJORDANINCPUBLISHING.COM • TVGUESTPERT.COM

ALSO PUBLISHED BY JACQUIE JORDAN INC.

Alex Detail's Rebellion
sequel to
Alex Detail's Revolution
by Darren Campo

Alex Detail is being assassinated.

Again.

The second Harvester war has ended, but Alex has never been in greater peril. Not only is Alex being hunted by his deadly clone, the seven-year-old George Spell, he is also the target of a House of Nations plot to expose Alex's post-war experiments with The Harvesters and disgrace the genius war hero.

But when George Spell's latest attempt to assassinate Alex Detail at the New York planetarium nearly kills hundreds of people, Alex escapes death only to find his would-be assassin suddenly kidnapped by the powerful mystic, Brother Lonadoon.

Now Alex must join Captain Odessa on a covert interplanetary rescue operation where they uncover clues left thousands of years ago by an ancient race desperately trying to send a message to the future. But the message might be too late, as phenomena are revealing the beginnings of an extinction level event caused by the ongoing war between Alex Detail and George Spell, one that could lead to the destruction of the entire solar system.

JACQUIEJORDANINCPUBLISHING.COM • TVGUESTPERT.COM

ALSO PUBLISHED BY JACQUIE JORDAN INC.

Beyond Cosmic Dice: Moral Life in a Random World

by Dr. Jeff Schweitzer and Giuseppe Nortarbartolo-di-Sciara

This is the book that ties it all together – the problems that religion creates in solving our looming problems, and the unholy environmental mess we're in. I'd say that someday we're going to have to listen to this man, but the truth is, that day is NOW.

— Bill Maher

Morality is our biological destiny. We each have within us the awesome power to create our own meaning in life, our own sense of purpose, our own destiny. With a natural ethic we are able to move beyond the random hand of birth to pave our own road to a better life. Whereas religion claims that happiness is found from submission to a higher power, a natural ethic defines happiness as the freedom to discover within ourselves our inherent good, and then to act on that better instinct, not because of any mandate from above or in obedience to the Bible, but because we can. With the ability to choose to be good comes the obligation to make that choice; choosing to be moral is what makes us special as individuals and as a species. With a natural ethic we free ourselves from the arbitrary and destructive constraints of divine interference to create a path toward a full life for which we ourselves are responsible.

JACQUIEJORDANINCPUBLISHING.COM • TVGUESTPERT.COM

ALSO PUBLISHED BY JACQUIE JORDAN INC.

The New Moral Code

Also titled
*Beyond Cosmic Dice:
Moral Life in a Random World,*
with a new introduction.

**by Dr. Jeff Schweitzer
and Giuseppe
Nortarbartolo-di-Sciara**

In a confusing world in which faith no longer satisfies, *The New Moral Code* paves a clear path to happiness and fulfillment. The authors provide simple and easy steps to free you from the angst of today's modern society. Learn to shed the burden of expectation created by others and pave your own road to a meaningful life of deep contentment.

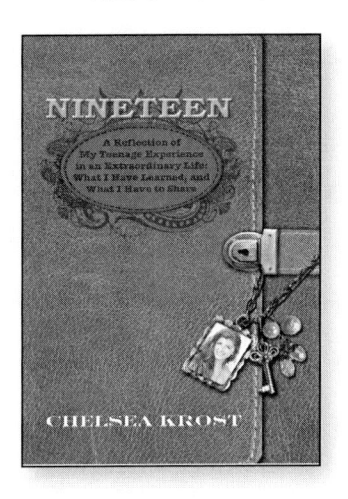

ALSO PUBLISHED BY JACQUIE JORDAN INC.

**NINETEEN
A Reflection of My Teenage Experience in an Extraordinary Life: What I Have Learned, and What I Have to Share**

by Chelsea Krost

In *NINETEEN: A Reflection of My Teenage Experience in an Extraordinary Life: What I Have Learned, and What I Have to Share*, nineteen-year-old author, Chelsea Krost, authentically shares the simplicity and complexity of her coming of age experience.

In NINETEEN, she conjures the curiosity and flavor of a personal journal left open in a teenager's room. In its direct approach, NINETEEN reveals the key events that teenagers face at this monumental time in their lives as experienced by Chelsea Krost. While many teens are struggling with typical angst from cat fights to cliques, many others are dealing with the downside of the advanced technological world we live in. From sexting to cyber bullying, self-esteem to depression; body image, mean girls and boy trouble,

Chelsea sheds light on the millennial mindset and its ever changing challenges and lightning speed curve balls.

Chelsea Krost is a nineteen year old radio talk show host and millennial spokesperson who has embarked on a new career as an author, sharing her inspirations, life lessons, motivation, and a voice for her peers, all through her own personal experiences and open diary.

JACQUIEJORDANINCPUBLISHING.COM • TVGUESTPERT.COM

ALSO PUBLISHED BY JACQUIE JORDAN INC.

The Real Purpose of Parenting: The Book You Wish Your Parents Read

Dr. Philip B. Dembo
"AMERICA'S PARENT COACH"

THE REAL PURPOSE OF PARENTING is a series of stories and life lessons from the world of a therapist, known as The Parent Coach. Very well-intentioned, well meaning parents are at the point of crisis with their kids because their own best parenting efforts are NOT producing the children they want them to be. And there, according to Dr. Phil Dembo, lies the problem.

In THE REAL PURPOSE OF PARENTING, even the best parents are capable of smothering the growth of their kid's life. This can happen because the truth of who the child is, and what the child truly needs is often overlooked or ignored in the agenda that many parents lay out for their kids. Thus ... often landing the family in a colossal melt down.

Dr. Dembo shows simple family "turn around" strategies that reframe the real purpose of parenting and gives each family, and child their own salvation.

JACQUIEJORDANINCPUBLISHING.COM • TVGUESTPERT.COM

BOOKS BY JACQUIE JORDAN

Get on TV!
The Insider's Guide to Pitching the Producers and Promoting Yourself

Expert advice on how to get booked and asked back!

"Jacquie ought to know how to get you on TV . . . she's put half the country on TV, including me."
– Maury Povich

In *Get on TV!*, Jacquie Jordan brings her expert advice straight to you – the entrepreneurs, experts, authors, and future reality stars looking to land a television spot. Jacquie shows you the ins and outs of the TV business and what you need to do to get booked (and asked back), including:

- The importance of tape and materials
- Speaking the language of the television producer
- Being persistent without being annoying
- What to do when you're booked and cancelled
- How to get asked back again and again

If you know the right moves, you can get on TV!

"Jacquie has the ability to maintain a fair balance between the voice of the project she is producing and the needs of her guests."
– John Edward, psychic medium and author of *Crossing Over*, host of John Edward: Cross Country

Jacquie Jordan has been involved in booking, supervising or producing over 10,000 television guests, as well as coaching countless people on how to get on air.

BOOKS BY JACQUIE JORDAN

Heartfelt Marketing Allowing the Universe to be Your Business Partner

Heartfelt Marketing is for the self-inspired entrepreneur who understands their skill set; however, promotion isn't their forte.

- Learn how to get out of your own way and generate business by being of service to others.
- Release the 5 Pitfalls that spell doom for your revenue.
- Discover how the language and intention make a HUGE difference in the sale.
- Let go of the energetic tackiness in your business exchanges that screams inferiority.
- Explore the blocks that are getting in the way of business expansion.

"The skills Jacquie taught me in her book, course, and coaching have given me the keys to successfully communicate to a broad audience in a language that catches attention but never compromises the core of the meaning of my work and mission in life. This is the alchemy of heart-based marketing; turning your invisible passionate emotions about your work, topic, or product, and turning it into a sound-track that will grab attention and invite a wide audience into your mission."
– Christine Stevens, UpBeat Drum Circles

"Jacquie Jordan sends a heartfelt message that we can be strong in business and still come from the Heart. This book represents where business is going – from being a one-track money model to an expression of who we are and one that can help humanity as well."
– Ali Brown, Ali International LLC, millionaire entrepreneur coach

ABOUT THE AUTHOR

One look at **Eve Michaels** and you are acutely aware that she cares about her appearance from the top of her glossy auburn hair to the tip of her elegant patent leather stiletto pumps. She cares so much about appearances that she has made a lifelong career out of helping others improve theirs.

Eve's introduction to the world of beauty was born out of her early childhood years of tragedy, when her mother suffered permanent brain damage and was institutionalized for life as a result of a car accident. Eve's intention to "heal" her mother came in shades of pink and red; the hues of make-up she used trying to restore her mother's beauty so she could be normal and hopefully come home to stay. Realizing the impact that this had on her life led to a mission to change America's perception and reflection of beauty, both inwardly and outwardly.

Eve Michaels has spent over thirty years in the business as an internationally acclaimed "Transformational Makeover Expert" and the creator of the Fast Track To Fabulous™ program.

A nationally recognized author and motivational speaker who captivate audiences globally, Eve teaches people life changing, easy-to-follow skills that quickly transform their image and their attitude about dressing well. Eve has an engaging and relatable gift for helping her clients understand what makes them special and how to create the right image that communicates their unique abilities and talents. It is no wonder her work is often called "Makeover Magic!" Her soft voice, compelling scenarios, edgy delivery and "walk the walk" style make for an entertaining escape into a new dimension of beauty and inspiration.

"We are playing in a global economy, and cannot be isolationists. We need to bring back style and image to look like world-class leaders once again."